Advising on Organisational Development in Education

An excellent point of reference for prospective, new or experienced education advisers and leaders, which focuses on organisational development in education.

Divided into three parts, the book explores the specifics of advising on organisational development in the context of change, planning for organisational effectiveness, and the impact of leadership on performance. It presents a diverse range of perspectives from multi-academy trust (MAT) leaders, headteachers, key influencers and education advisers working at local, regional, national, and international levels. Many of the chapters focus on real case work and conclude with the authors' analyses of impact, resulting in a thorough, insightful and practical guide for those working in an advisory capacity with education leaders. Case scenarios also encourage readers to reflect on and consider applying some of these approaches in their own practice. Chapters address key aspects of:

- empowering leaders through effective organisational development
- future-proofing your organisation
- responding to and working with political change
- making change work for your organisation
- the importance of governance in sustaining organisational development
- organisational development within the school setting

Readers, throughout the book, are encouraged to understand more fully the intricacies of organisational effectiveness, enabling them to further hone their advisory skillset and support leaders in continuing to improve the quality of education for all children and young people.

The vision of the Association of Education Advisers (AoEA) is that every school, college and education provider has access to high-quality support, advice and challenge, which is independent and focused on improving outcomes for children, schools and their communities.

The AoEA's mission is to provide an accredited quality standard, to support continuous professional learning aligned to the standard and to create an international community for those who support schools, colleges and other education providers.

The Education Adviser

About the Book Series

The Education Adviser series covers all aspects of the education advisory role inclusive of focusing on: the skills required of an adviser; enabling effective support for school improvement; governance; change management; organisational development; and quality systems. It provides the most up-to-date thinking with examples of some exemplary practice from across the UK and internationally. Contributions include chapters selected from a pool of some 500 AoEA-accredited associates and partners, as well as some well-known education specialists in their field.

Series Editor and Author: The AoEA

Books in this series include:

The Role of the Education Adviser
Advising on School Improvement
Advising on Governance in Education
Advising on Organisational Development in Education

Two further books soon to be published, entitled *Advising on Change Management in Education* and *Advising on Quality Systems in Education*, will complete the series.

For more information about this series, please visit: https://www.routledge.com/The-Education-Adviser/book-series/CRITTEA

Advising on Organisational Development in Education

Produced by
the Association of Education Advisers

ASSOCIATION
of EDUCATION
ADVISERS

Routledge
Taylor & Francis Group

LONDON AND NEW YORK

Designed cover image: Out of House Limited and Getty Images

First published 2026
by Routledge
4 Park Square, Milton Park, Abingdon, Oxon OX14 4RN

and by Routledge
605 Third Avenue, New York, NY 10158

Routledge is an imprint of the Taylor & Francis Group, an informa business

© 2026 Association of Education Advisers

The right of the Association of Education Advisers to be identified as authors of this work has been asserted in accordance with sections 77 and 78 of the Copyright, Designs and Patents Act 1988.

All rights reserved. No part of this book may be reprinted or reproduced or utilised in any form or by any electronic, mechanical, or other means, now known or hereafter invented, including photocopying and recording, or in any information storage or retrieval system, without permission in writing from the publishers.

Trademark notice: Product or corporate names may be trademarks or registered trademarks, and are used only for identification and explanation without intent to infringe.

For Product Safety Concerns and Information please contact our EU representative GPSR@taylorandfrancis.com. Taylor & Francis Verlag GmbH, Kaufingerstraße 24, 80331 München, Germany.

British Library Cataloguing-in-Publication Data
A catalogue record for this book is available from the British Library

ISBN: 978-1-041-10457-5 (hbk)
ISBN: 978-1-041-10454-4 (pbk)
ISBN: 978-1-003-65517-6 (ebk)

DOI: 10.4324/9781003655176

Typeset in Montserrat
by Apex CoVantage, LLC

The purpose of this book, as one of a series of six, is to support the professional learning of those who are involved in education and in providing support to others, including (i) those currently engaged as leaders in educational settings; and, (ii) those who are advising and supporting them.

Contents

About the editorial team	ix
About the contributors	xii
Acknowledgements	xviii

Overview

Introduction to the AoEA and the purpose of the book series Les Walton CBE	3
Introduction to Book 4: *Advising on Organisational Development in Education* Dr Tony Birch	6

Part 1: Advising on organisational development in the context of change

1	Future-proofing your organisation with PESTLE Ian Lane	21
2	Responding to and working with political change: the art of the possible Sir Peter Lauener CB	32
3	Advising on organisational development in a fast-changing technological context Al Kingsley MBE	40
4	Managing the risks of structural change Joanne Davison	51
5	Beyond comfort zones: advising on organisational development in turbulent times Catherine Redgrave	57
6	Continuing to develop as an outstanding initial teacher training provider in the context of significant national change Liz Birchinall	64
7	Developing the quality of SEND provision across a system of schools: A Northern Ireland case study Kirsty Logan-Hall	73

Part 2: Planning for organisational effectiveness

8	The importance of the strategic plan in aligning planning, people and performance Peter Parish	83

9	Developing an effective, compassionate and inclusive curriculum *Narinder Gill*	95
10	Advising on the management of effective and sustainable curriculum design *Kevin McDermid*	106
11	A perspective on recruiting an effective senior leadership team *Roisin Harbinson*	114
12	Advising schools in areas of significant, socio-economic disadvantage *Sian Smith*	124
13	The responsibilities of governance in ensuring a sustained, strategic focus on organisational development *Emma Knights OBE*	133

Part 3: The impact of leadership on performance

14	The importance of ethical leadership in organisational development *Carolyn Roberts*	145
15	Assessing the impact of leadership on the Context for Organisational Improvement (COI) *Les Walton CBE, Peter Parish and Ian Lane*	152
16	Empowering leaders through effective organisational development *Matthew Humphreys*	161
17	Enabling a structured approach to collaboration across a diverse system of schools in Northern Ireland *Catherine Wegwermer MBE, Harry Greer, Damian Eannetta and Jackie Wallace*	169
18	Building bridges: a case study in supporting 'deputes' to become headteachers *Grant Gillies*	179
19	Transforming education through visionary leadership and effective organisational development *Les Walton CBE*	189

Conclusions

Reflections on Book 4: *Advising on Organisational Development in Education* *Dr Tony Birch and Ian Lane*	196

Index	206

About the editorial team

Dr Tony Birch, Series Editor

Tony is author of *Understanding Primary Education as a Whole* and Founding Director of Birch Education, an educational consultancy dedicated to empowering individuals and teams to develop high-quality, sustainable approaches. Previously, Tony worked for Bolton Council for more than 20 years: as a school improvement adviser and head of school improvement before becoming the lead for education and learning strategy.

Ian Lane, Chair of the Editorial Team

Following headship of an inner-city secondary school, Ian joined a local authority advisory service as a senior adviser and was later appointed Director of School Improvement for the same 'core city'. In more recent years, he has held CEO roles in both a primary and a secondary schools' multi-academy trust and worked as an independent school improvement adviser.

Les Walton CBE, Executive Chair of the AoEA

Les' career spans pivotal changes in education since the 1960s. His book, *Education the Rock and Roll Years,* is described by Professor Andy Hargreaves as 'visionary . . . An excellent piece of writing'. Les has been a headteacher, director of education and principal of a further education college. He has also had significant regional and national influence. He founded Northern Education Associates and Schools North-East. Nationally, he chaired the Young People's Learning Agency and assisted its transition to the Education and Skills Funding Agency. He has also been a key adviser to multiple UK Secretaries of State. Les received the OBE in 1996 and CBE in 2013 for his services to education.

Eric Halton, former Head of School Improvement, Hampshire

Over a period of 13 years, Eric's leadership in primary headships significantly improved curriculum, teaching and leadership capacity, resulting in inclusive provision and high quality outcomes for all children. During this time, he also held a number of school-to-school system roles as consultant to individual schools, building professional practice networks. Eric, in more recent years, was head of a highly regarded school improvement service working in all sectors.

Eithne Leming, School Improvement Consultant

Eithne has worked as an education adviser and consultant since 2007. Her work includes school improvement work for the National Strategies and academy trusts and for a range of maintained primary and special schools. She has held local authority roles for Special Educational Needs and Disabilities (SEND), Looked After Children and for primary assessment as KS1/2 moderation manager. She is a highly skilled school improvement adviser and coach.

Mary Lowery, Head of School Improvement, Northern Ireland

Mary has over 20 years' teaching experience in two urban integrated comprehensive colleges in Derry and Belfast and has been part of the development of integrated education in Northern Ireland since its early days. Mary joined the Education and Training Inspectorate (ETI) in 2014, inspecting across educational phases and supporting the development of models of inspection and self-evaluation, before moving into school development work with the Education Authority in 2018. In 2019, she co-founded WomenEdNI, which connects and inspires women in educational leadership.

Mairéad Mhig Uaid, School and System Improvement, Northern Ireland

Mairéad has 20 years' experience in school senior leadership, bringing about both school and system-wide improvement. Her experience extends beyond organisational settings to the design and delivery of tailored curriculum, resource and teacher professional learning. Mairéad leads school and system improvement through a people-centric coaching style.

Peter Parish, AoEA Development Team

Peter formerly led a school improvement service in a local authority in the North-East of England. During this time, the council was awarded Beacon Council status for 'Tackling School Failure'. He also co-ordinated successful funding proposals for major education projects. He then became Head of Planning, Commissioning and Quality Assurance in the council's Children's Services. In 2010, he became Director of Operations for Northern Education Associates.

Megan Liebnitz, AoEA Central Team

After graduating with a masters in English literature, Megan joined the AoEA in January 2024 to run their accreditation programme for all senior educational leaders. She makes sure that the programme runs efficiently and that all candidates have access to support they may need throughout the process. Megan also helps support professional learning and monthly Education Keeping In Touch (EduKIT) meetings throughout the academic year, with help from members of the AoEA Assessment Team and external specialists.

About the contributors

Liz Birchinall, Director of Primary PGCE, University of Manchester

Liz Birchinall, Reader in Education and Programme Director of Primary Postgraduate Certificate in Education (PGCE) at Manchester University, brings 20+ years of teaching excellence across primary and secondary sectors. A Senior Fellow of the Higher Education Academy with multiple advanced degrees (MSc Ed Research, BSc Science, PGCE, NPQH), she previously served as a school vice-principal. Under her leadership, the PGCE programme has achieved consecutive outstanding Ofsted ratings. Her award-winning work focuses on teacher well-being, mindfulness and AI in education.

Joanne Davison, Partner, Muckle LLP

Joanne has advised education organisations for over 20 years on a range of legal issues and has personally led in excess of 800 academy conversion/transfer projects and mergers in the sector over recent years. Joanne's knowledgeable and friendly approach alongside her technical expertise has led her to be a trusted adviser, and she regularly advises boards and senior leadership teams on a range of strategic issues including collaborative working and restructuring. Joanne also regularly speaks at internal and external training events.

Damian Eannetta, School Improvement Professional, Northern Ireland

Damian is a school improvement professional and experienced educational leader with a strong commitment to equity, aspiration and collaborative practice. Through his work with the Education Authority, he has led strategic initiatives including the *Pathways Into Partnership* programme and the *Drawing the Future* study. Damian's work focuses on developing effective partnership approaches and embedding career-related learning in the primary phase, helping to shape policy and broaden children's horizons from an early age.

Narinder Gill, DfE RISE Adviser and recent MAT Director for School Improvement

Currently serving as a Department for Education (DfE) RISE Adviser supporting school improvement in England, Narinder was recently the Director of School Improvement for Elevate Primary Trust in North Yorkshire. She has over 30 years of experience in education, having successfully led three schools as headteacher. Her leadership at her last school is documented in her book *Creating Change in Urban Settings*. Narinder is also a strategic director with the Curriculum Foundation, leading on international curriculum development, most recently in South Sudan. She is also a qualified and practising executive coach.

Grant Gillies, Headteacher, City of Edinburgh, UK

Grant Gillies is Headteacher of South Morningside Primary in Edinburgh. He has worked at national level, with the General Teaching Council of Scotland and Education Scotland, and has been principal of a range of successful 3–18 British International Schools abroad. He continues to work with the Council of British International Schools and is an accredited associate with the Association of Educational Advisers.

Harry Greer, Former School Principal, now Education Consultant, Northern Ireland

With extensive experience of primary school leadership and 10 years as a board member and chair of leading peacebuilding charity (Community Relations in Schools), Harry has been a passionate advocate for children and those who work with them. Having also held key roles within the National Association of Headteachers, he has a strong vision for improvement, practical support and the power of collaboration. *Pathways Into Partnership* was his first piece of work as an associate with the Education Authority NI.

Roisin Harbinson, Senior Education Adviser, Northern Ireland

Roisin is a passionate advocate for high-quality leadership training that incorporates coaching, positive mindset and personal well-being. With extensive experience in education, holding roles as vice-principal and principal in post primary, she has dedicated her life to enhancing leadership practices at all levels. She recently founded 'MarbleMinds', a leadership development and coaching consultancy. Holding an MA in education and MSc in mindfulness and trained in acceptance and commitment therapy (ACT), she has delivered the mindfulness-based stress education (MBSR) programme for school principals in the maintained sector.

Matthew Humphreys, Improvement Officer, Rhondda Cynon Taf County Borough Council, Wales

Matthew is a senior associate with the AoEA, an experienced school leader and improvement professional. He has held leadership positions in a broad range of settings across Wales. He currently works with schools to support improvement during a time of significant reform. Additionally, Matthew provides professional learning on effective self-evaluation and governance across the region. Matthew was previously responsible for digital learning, contributing to national policy and professional learning.

Al Kingsley MBE, Chair of a Multi-Academy Trust and Education Adviser

Al has spent the last 35 years in the educational technology space, and 20 of those have been spent as a school trustee and governor. He was awarded an MBE in the King's 2025 New Year's Honours for services to education. He is Chair of Hampton Academies Trust in the East of England. Al also sits on the Department for Education's Regional Schools Directors Advisory Board for the East of England and is the independent chair of Peterborough's SEND Board.

Emma Knights OBE, former CEO of the National Governance Association

Emma Knights was Chief Executive of the National Governance Association from 2010 to 2024, growing its services and the understanding of school and trust governance. She had the privilege of representing the voice of school governors and academy trustees across England. Her learning from that role is being published as the *Power of Governance* in early 2026. Before the NGA, Emma worked in third-sector organisations, always aiming to support people from disadvantaged backgrounds with advocacy, access to civil rights and entitlements, tackling child poverty or encouraging early education.

Sir Peter Lauener CB, former Chief Executive of the Education and Skills Funding Agency

Sir Peter Lauener, knighted for his services to education, has previously held the roles of Chief Executive of the Education and Skills Funding Agency (ESFA), interim Chief Executive of the Institute for Apprenticeships and then interim Chief Executive of the Student Loans Company. Peter now has a number of non-executive roles. He was appointed as Chair of the Construction Industry Training Board in May 2018 and Chair of the Student Loans Company in April 2020. Peter is also the Chair of Orchard Hill College, an independent special needs college based in South and West London.

Kirsty Logan-Hall, Principal of Tullygally Primary School, Northern Ireland

Kirsty is an advocate for special educational needs and early intervention who believes that hands-on professional learning is essential for effective professional growth and capacity-building. Following various leadership roles, she is now the principal of a primary school which has been transformed in recent years. She works closely with the education authority and Department of Education to ensure that learning pathways for all children are successful. She supports and advises other schools on 'transformation', not only for the children but also for the staff and the community.

Kevin McDermid, AoEA Development Team

Kevin has over 25 years of senior leadership experience in secondary schools, including headships of two inner-city comprehensive schools, and the principalship of a sixth-form college. He was Teaching Awards Head Teacher of the Year for the North-East and Cumbria in 2004–5 and has latterly served as CEO of a multi-academy trust. Kevin has extensive experience as a school improvement adviser and independent consultant. Over the last fifteen years, he has worked with many individual schools across the UK and numerous LAs and multi-academy trusts in England.

Catherine Redgrave, School Improvement Manager, Hampshire County Council

Catherine has worked as a school improvement adviser in Hampshire since 2009. A former headteacher, she supports leadership development, teaching quality and assessment across schools. Her work includes co-ordinating and innovating support for schools where required, and she is the strategic lead for inclusion and diversity work across the county. Her MA(Ed) focused on engaging parents through action research. Catherine is passionate about developing leadership at all levels and works closely with teachers, leaders and governors.

Carolyn Roberts, Secretary of the Ethical Leadership Alliance

Carolyn was a comprehensive school headteacher for 23 years and ASCL Honorary Secretary for 4. During that time, she chaired the Ethical Leadership Commission and is now secretary of its successor, the Ethical Leadership Alliance. She co-wrote *Knowledge and the Future School* with Michael Young (2014) and is author of *Ethical Leadership for a Better Education System* (2019). Carolyn is Co-Director of The Professional Teaching Institute (PTI), the independent education charity set up by HM The King 20 years ago, for whom she is co-editing a series of books.

Sian Smith, Primary Phase Inspector, Hampshire County Council

Sian is an experienced education professional who has devoted the majority of her career to working in schools facing significant social and economic disadvantage. Her background includes roles as a local authority teaching and learning adviser, headteacher, consultant headteacher, and executive headteacher. Currently, Sian serves as a primary phase inspector and education adviser for Hampshire county council. She is passionate about supporting schools in challenging circumstances, helping to drive improvement and foster positive outcomes for pupils and communities.

Jackie Wallace, former School Principal, now Education Consultant, Northern Ireland

Jackie has worked in education for over 40 years. A former school inspector and a member of the Education and Training Inspectorate's Mathematics Panel, he has also been the principal of three primary schools. He is passionate about empowering local school leaders to affect change and improvement. Since his retirement in 2021, Jackie has worked as an education consultant on a wide range of projects and reviews.

Catherine Wegwermer MBE, former School Principal, now Education Consultant, Northern Ireland

As a former principal, Catherine brings a wealth of practical experience to her role as a coach and mentor for other school leaders. While working as a consultant, Catherine has supported schools to drive meaningful improvement. As an associate with the Education Authority NI, she has contributed to significant research, most recently completing the *Pathways Into Partnership Framework*. Her dedication and impact on the educational landscape have been recognised with the award of an MBE for Services to Education.

Acknowledgements

The development of the AoEA book series has been an important milestone for the Association and this fourth book focuses on advising on organisational development in education. The range of chapters capture the innovative work of our associates and friends of our organisation but they crystallise the journey of the AoEA which has included the construction of criteria, establishing processes of accreditation and widespread professional learning and conversation. This book from a wide range of perspectives captures the energy, debates and approaches at the heart of advisory work specifically in relation to organisational development.

With this in mind, I'd like to extend my thanks to the editorial team, to each of our authors and to the publishing team who, in a short period of time, have contributed to bringing this book to publication. A huge amount of energy, reflection and craft has gone into creating such an engaging and varied text which is hugely appreciated.

Les Walton CBE
Executive Chair of the AoEA

Introduction to the AoEA and the purpose of the book series

LES WALTON CBE

As we move deeper into the third decade of the 21st century, the need to re-design the process by which schools are supported and enabled to improve has become increasingly important. In 2016, a meeting was held in the Department for Education headquarters in London. Key national school and college representative organisations were present. All agreed that there was a need to quality assure and develop the quality of advice and support that schools receive.

Following an intensive research and development programme, it was decided to establish the Association of Education Advisers (AoEA), which is independent of national and local government. It was also decided that the AoEA should provide an accredited international standard that would be relevant to all schools, colleges and education providers across the UK and, ultimately, throughout the world.

The AoEA has a vision that every school and college, no matter their size or designation, has access to high-quality support, advice and challenge, which is independent and focused on improving outcomes for children and young people, their schools, their colleges and their communities.

There are 36,000 schools across the UK alone. The core message from those who support and advise on school improvement to those who lead and inspect is that we should 'professionalise' the role of the adviser. A major part of the work of the AoEA has been in developing the professional community within the UK and internationally for those who support and advise schools, colleges and other education providers.

This accredited national and international community of advisers is increasing by the day. We believe that we are at the very beginning of our journey. While at the outset we seriously underestimated the potential of an international community of education advisers, we don't anymore!

We believe that those who lead, inspect and advise schools should have access to accredited standards and continuous professional learning. The three points of this triangular relationship are all necessary. If one part is weakened, then the whole system becomes unsustainable.

Advising and supporting colleagues within schools and colleges over which you may not have direct power and control requires a unique set of skills and knowledge. The hundreds of educationalists who have achieved the AoEA-accredited standard tell us that they value most highly the independent nature of the AoEA, the opportunity to reflect on their work through a rigorous accreditation process and associated professional learning. They tell us that the AoEA process provides:

- an opportunity to reflect on their own practice through external eyes, condense and showcase their contribution to organisational improvement;
- a valuable opportunity to receive external affirmation and feedback, whilst also having signposted opportunities for further learning.

It helps them to:

- validate their ability to advise others;
- understand their own skills and expertise in relation to how they can support others;
- develop further and hone their skills and expertise in supporting others;
- make others aware of their knowledge, skills and experience, thereby strengthening the educational advisory network and potential for increased learning and support from one another.

In harnessing the strengths of our growing membership, this series of books, titled 'The Education Adviser', will provide some of the most up-to-date thinking and examples of good practice from across the UK and internationally. If you provide advice and support or lead a school and college, then the aim of this series of books is to provide some essential reading. The AoEA has selected contributors from the 500-plus accredited AoEA Associates and partners together with well-known experts from across the UK and beyond.

All contributors have mastery in their specific area, whether it is in demonstrating professional credibility, understanding what causes a school's success or failure, developing a school improvement strategy, supporting major change programmes or using quality improvement tools such as Kaizen.

The books in the series are as follows:

1. *The Role of the Education Adviser*
2. *Advising on School Improvement*
3. *Advising on Governance in Education*
4. *Advising on Organisational Development in Education*
5. *Advising on Change Management in Education*
6. *Advising on Implementing Quality Systems in Education*

This book, *Advising on Organisational Development in Education*, is the fourth in our series. We hope you will enjoy reading it and that it contributes to your professional learning and work as an education adviser wherever you may be working in supporting and advising school and college leaders.

Introduction to Book 4: *Advising on Organisational Development in Education*

DR TONY BIRCH

For the Association of Education Advisers (AoEA) organisational development (OD) is a planned and systematic approach to achieving the desired goals of high performance and continuous improvement across an organisation through the alignment of strategy, people and processes (AoEA, 2025). This first book in the Senior Associate part of the series explores the role of the adviser in relation to this.

OD involves complex, varied and interrelated approaches to 'strategy', 'people', 'processes' and 'performance': 'strategy', for example, includes the setting of aims, the art of planning and directing the development of an organisation; the 'people' dimension includes leadership, values, professional learning, structure and job design; 'processes' include systems, policies and operations, while 'performance' considers how effectively the organisation meets its aims and goals.

Organisational development in context

Educational organisations never exist in vacuums and develop and change to reflect their socio-cultural context. If we delve, briefly, into history we can see this in play: Joan Simon's classic study of the Tudor period noted how powerful societal changes impacted on educational organisations: the effects of charitable endowments, new ideas (especially humanism), the changing concept of the state, increased use of the vernacular, and technical advance, especially printing (Simon, 1966), all accelerated development.

Organisations develop over time: new priorities emerge, policies change, requirements and expectations evolve, opportunities surface and threats may appear to which leaders and their organisations respond. Emma Knights' chapter (2025), for example, exemplifies this in relation to the changing nature, demands and processes of governance in the English education system. This impact is evidenced internationally, too, for example, in Robin Alexander's (2000) extensive exploration of culture and pedagogy in England, France, India, Russia and the United States, and, more recently, in Lucy Crehan's (2016) educational travelogue, both of which revealed the ways in which culturally specific elements of jurisdictions create education systems that have unique organisational forms. Education systems and the organisations within them have distinctive identities and vary when compared one with another (Archer, 1984).

The myriad of social influences on schools continue to evolve. Note, for example, the impact of new technologies: in the last 30 years, the world wide web, powerful mobile devices and, now, artificial intelligence have shaped and reshaped education. The recent debate around mobile phones in schools illustrates the continuing demands on organisations to respond (Beck, 2024).

OD is a continuous process in today's fast changing world: Yrjö Engeström's research group at the University of Helsinki, for example, recognised that organisations now undergo cycles of qualitative changes more frequently than before (see Engeström, 1987).

Organisational development in action

While OD may have external drivers, it is equally the case that it has a starting point within the organisation itself: it is a planned and systematic process where people generate action, positively affecting their environment while relating to their wider context. In this respect, strategy, at an organisational level, is, in part, how organisations respond internally to what transpires externally.

Each organisation has its own 'ecology': subtle and unique differences in the relationships and connections that make its components (its history, strategy, people, processes and performance) distinctive. There are many elements to this: safeguarding systems, human resource management, financial planning and monitoring, the many dimensions of governance, stakeholder engagement, among many others, even before mentioning the essential core of pedagogy, curriculum and assessment. Educational organisations are in a constant process of evolution with many moving parts. John Macbeath captured this particularly well in *Schools Must Speak for Themselves*:

> *Conflict, dilemma and ambiguity are, of course, at the very centre of learning, individual and organisational, and it is this constant grappling with complexity that makes schools interesting and dynamic places. Effective schools, in their myriad forms, never stay still long enough to be pinned down.*
> (MacBeath, 1999, p. 9)

Understanding that ecology, too, means consciously exploring plans, decisions and actions in advance of implementing them, considering their effects and any potential unintended consequences.

Leadership becomes a critical dimension of OD and educational research consistently confirms its importance (Leithwood et al., 2019): it embraces the notion of human agency – our ability to influence and shape our environment through vision, values and direction. Leadership enables organisations to transcend Henry Ford's aphorism that '*if you always do what you've always done, you'll always get what you always got*'. There is constant development and finding of the right process for development whether that be minor adaptations, attention to alignment of processes, strategic redesign or urgent reactive action. Identifying the right levers and choosing the most appropriate 'active ingredients' requires judgement and skill.

The role of the organisational development adviser (ODA)

OD might be seen as a search for congruence: the sense in which the aims, purpose and values of an organisation, its pedagogy and curriculum, its professionals, the organisational systems and the culture synchronise. The ODA guides and supports educational organisations in bringing this to fruition: they work closely with leaders in identifying priorities and approaches that are context-specific and of high value using a repertoire of skills – including coaching, facilitating and professional learning tailored to need. When issues are identified, they search for clarity and identify causal factors, seeking to resolve them creatively and productively.

The AoEA criteria reflect what is needed from the ODA in education. This repertoire includes:

- understanding the PESTLE drivers for change;
- critically evaluating the design of the curriculum or educational offer;
- linking vision, policy, strategy, plans, goals and ambitions to long-term and immediate needs;
- linking job design and people development to strategic requirements;
- analysing management procedures and systems;
- selecting and applying a variety of measurements of success and performance indicators;
- assessing the impact of leadership on the context for organisational improvement.

The ODA has three areas of focus:

Understanding and analysing context. ODAs delve into the complexities of organisations and systems and understand the wider societal and cultural context: they balance the ability to be forensic when necessary, addressing detail, yet they have a wider view, looking holistically at the organisation, carefully understanding the layers of interrelating processes and people.

Planning for organisational effectiveness. The ODA is skilled in recognising immediate and pressing challenges, establishing priorities and focusing action where needed to immediate effect, but they also see the long-term picture, recognising that sustainable approaches (this might be, for example, in relation to workload) are vital for the continued success and the continued 'health' of the organisation.

Understanding the impact of leadership. Leaders can be transformational, bringing about meaningful and sustainable change with tangible benefits for children and young people. This is an optimistic version of human activity: ODAs support leaders by empowering and enabling, by encouraging a repertoire of approaches that are fit for purpose from leaders who are ethical, reflective and generous.

The ODA has a key role to play in shaping the strategic and operational response to changing demands: they draw from a range of diagnostic tools, such as PESTLE (political, economic, social, technological, legal, environmental analysis) or Ishikawa (fishbone diagrams), which explores the causes of a specific problem, alongside developmental, planning and project management methods.

Structure of the book

This book explores the ODA role, from a range of perspectives, in various contexts (including contributions from England, Northern Ireland, Scotland and Wales) demonstrating the rich complexity of educational systems and how the skilled ODA can support processes of continuous, substantive and sustainable development.

To showcase the examples, this book is divided into three parts: (i) advising on organisational development in a changing context, (ii) planning for organisational effectiveness and (iii) understanding the impact of leadership in organisational development.

Part 1: Advising on organisational development in a changing context

Strategy must involve an organisation responding internally to what transpires around them: namely, the political, economic, social, technological, legal and environmental (commonly known as PESTLE) landscape, each dimension of which brings opportunities and threats for organisations. Ian Lane describes a structured process of analysing, identifying and evaluating these, explaining how these can inform an OD strategy which fits well with its values and current stage of development. Three chapters then explore aspects of PESTLE.

Firstly, the complexity of PESTLE is strongly present in Sir Peter Lauener's contribution which focuses primarily on the politics of education reflecting his experience in a national strategic role in England. It is a powerful illustration of how political drivers and decision-making have influenced the educational landscape. His message for the ODA includes understanding *'the key drivers in national education policy and discuss with any school you are supporting, how they are responding to national policy drivers'* before concluding with a reminder that *'education must effectively serve communities with purpose'*: he asks: *'is the school focused sufficiently on how it can help its pupils become confident, assured adults?'*

Secondly, Al Kingsley's account also explores another of the key PESTLE dimensions, namely, the impact of new technologies, including artificial intelligences, whose pace of development, at times, can feel breathtaking. He argues that education must engage with this fast-changing landscape but believes it is vital that they are scrutinised through the lenses of impact, equity and sustainability. This means two things: (i) clearly articulating why change is needed and how it aligns with an organisation's mission and (ii) ensuring staff feel valued, prepared and supported on their professional journeys. A key message for the ODA is to help organisations cultivate a culture of reflection and collaboration that reflects on successes and missteps.

Thirdly, from a legal perspective, Joanne Davison's chapter considers managing risk in organisational development. She argues that essential to the management of change are *'proper preparation, open communication, asking the right questions, challenging rationales and reminding leaders of the values and ethos that are guiding the change'*. She explains that lack of knowledge, direction and communication, alongside failure to make difficult decisions, can derail the process of change; therefore, the ODA can have a key role in helping leaders keep on track while navigating a myriad of issues and processes.

The external demands which PESTLE considers manifest in many different ways. Three practical examples of system and organisational responses now follow. In Catherine Redgrave's account she describes change across an education system (76 schools and 19,000 pupils) in response to *'a review into the lived experience of black and minority ethnic (BAME) communities in a large English town'*. She shows the value of an OD approach where there was clarity of vision relating to political and social drivers for change. The approach drew on the knowledge and expertise of colleagues to set goals and strategy, held influence through demonstrating commitment to the vision and used a variety of measures and planned performance indicators to reflect both short and long-term change – and, as she comments, *'the momentum is growing'*.

A quite different but equally practical example of responding to contextual changes is exemplified in Liz Birchenall's account. She describes the rapidly changing context of initial teacher education and its competing demands. A unique aspect of this case study is the complexity of managing multiple stakeholders and demands on the primary PGCE programme. She explains how Michael Fullan's model of change (initiation, implementation and continuation) enabled them to clarify their approach to respond so that their approach had *'fidelity with their programme vision'*. Ultimately, she offers three key messages: have robust self-evaluation processes, take ownership of delegated responsibilities and make a commitment to involve all stakeholders through regular and clear communication.

Kirsty Logan-Hall's example is set in the context of Special Educational Needs and Disabilities provision in Northern Ireland and, in particular, growing demand. Here we see the importance of developing a strategy that responds sensitively to context. The responsive approach recognises that a holistic approach is needed across the system to meet the needs of children and young people, first and foremost, and as close to their own communities as possible – and, consequently, creates a commitment to working in partnership with schools to build the physical and professional capacity to meet this need.

Collectively, this opening section highlights the ever-present process of change in education systems and how this can be navigated skilfully by attending to the wider socio-cultural context. However, there is a strong message, too, from all of the authors, that the vision, values and purpose of the organisation must hold the centre ground, guiding decisions and actions taken along the way.

Part 2: Planning for organisational effectiveness

Peter Parish opens the second section. His chapter describes a holistic model of organisational development: he offers a framework for designing an organisation through the alignment of its strategy, people and processes. The dimensions being: curriculum offered; strategy and development plans; structure, job design and policies; leadership and values; management, policies and systems; performance indicators; and the context for organisational improvement. He makes three key points:

- Strategic planning and improvement planning should always be sharply focused on delivering to the needs of the organisation.
- Leadership has a key role in setting the values of the organisation and in facilitating alignment.
- All strategic developments should take into account the capacity of the staff of the organisation to successfully deliver change.

There are strong elements of the OD framework described by Peter Parish illustrated in the next chapters. In Narinder Gill's account, set in the context of a multi-academy trust in England, leadership and values are to the fore. She describes the design of the curriculum as a *'moral and cultural act'* that shapes *'a culture of belonging, of hope, and of wisdom'*. Central to her proposition was her approach to organisational development which she describes thus: *'you must build a compelling moral case, provide structure, and then step back, creating conditions for others to lead'*.

Developing the curriculum means understanding context (people, place and environment); curriculum design principles; and co-creation within a guiding framework.

This is complemented by Kevin McDermid's chapter which focuses on the application of integrated curriculum and financial planning (ICFP) as a strategic approach to the design of a sustainable model for the curriculum. He explains how, through stages that involve ascertaining accurate student numbers, constructing a curriculum plan, staff deployment and benchmarking against others, it is possible to create a three-year integrated financial curriculum plan that matches the vision and principles of curriculum 'intent'.

Two chapters then demonstrate how an OD framework must be responsive to context. Roisin Harbinson, first, explores leadership. She recognises that an effective senior leadership team should be unique to the school it serves and that short-term effectiveness will not be sustainable if longer-term strategic approaches are not established. The design and development of such a team is key because, as she concludes:

> *Senior leadership teams are on a voyage together and before they set sail, they need a moral compass to address the storms ahead and a well mapped out route in the form of the strategic plan. The voyage may be long, so building relationships is crucial.*

Secondly, in England, and firmly grounding this section in practice, Sian Smith explains how she has advised a range of schools, all of which had in common socio-economic disadvantage. She shows how an emphasis on the development of 'people' is vital. She explains that when advisers enable leaders to transcend limiting beliefs from *'what else can you expect from our context'* to *'there are no limits to what we can achieve'* and equip teachers not just with a desire for improvement but what she describes as a 'bucketful' of knowledge and expertise, it is then that OD becomes most powerful in its impact on children and young people.

In concluding this section, it is important to recognise that planning for OD needs oversight and, thus, governance has a number of roles to play. Emma Knights argues in her chapter that the governing board should set a vision and a strategic direction which ensures the organisation's development and sustainability. Governance should consider a series of questions: Where are we now? What might be coming up next? What is our vision? What are the obstacles in our way? What are the strategic priorities? How will we know if we have achieved this vision? In summary, she comments:

> *The organisation's strategy needs to be communicated well, annually reviewed with stakeholders, and focus the work of both the board and the senior leadership.*

Collectively, these chapters are a reminder that the process of planning in organisations is an ongoing, often iterative process, but one that should combine the interrelating dimensions of strategy, people, processes and performance.

Part 3: The impact of leadership on performance

Leadership is a vital dimension of OD, and this section opens with two frameworks that can help to guide this. Carolyn Roberts account of ethical leadership is first. She presents seven 'virtues' or personal characteristics of ethical leadership (trust, wisdom, kindness, justice, service, courage, optimism) and describes this as a framework for leaders to reflect: advisers can use questions informed by the Framework for Ethical Leadership in Education (FELE) as part of their conversations about organisational development, securing the foundations for a principled approach. It leads into the next chapter, *Analysing the context for organisational development*, and a framework for this set out by Peter Parish, Ian Lane and Les Walton, which assesses and seeks to enhance the organisational environment through analysing data drawn from seven key dimensions: vision, policy, responsibility, achievement, recognition, relationships and sustainability. The authors argue that

> *By analysing these dimensions, leadership teams can identify areas for improvement and foster a working environment that supports professional growth and organisational success.*

A trilogy of contrasting and complementary chapters follow that focus on systems and illustrate the benefits of leadership approaches to school improvement where knowledge and expertise are shared between organisations and where collective responsibility is recognised. The first is set in the Welsh context where Matthew Humphreys describes how OD, in relation to the *Curriculum for Wales*, is an ongoing and systematic process that demands regular reflection on progress; he explains that this is needed at both school and system level so that there are shared understandings and priorities. He argues that the ODA is well-placed to support effective and collaborative OD in a complex and ever-changing education system. On a similar theme in relation to partnership working, Catherine Wegwermer, Harry Greer, Damian Eannetta and Jackie Wallace's exploration of collaboration through Northern Ireland's 'Pathways Into Partnership' programme identifies a number of key ingredients. They argue that structured but flexible frameworks and support systems are essential for successful partnerships to thrive, but it is also skilled 'collaborative leadership' that plays a crucial role in fostering their culture and sustaining them. Thirdly, in Scotland, Grant Gillies describes how, across a large education authority, he set out on a journey to support a key element of successful organisations – the development of leaders. His reflective account describes how he, with headteacher colleagues, set out to support deputy headteachers across a number of schools on their journey to the vital role of headship. These three chapters illustrate Fullan and Hargreaves' point: *'collective responsibility is not just a commitment; it is the exercise of capabilities on a deep and wide scale'* (Hargreaves & Fullan, 2012, p. 142).

The final chapter from Les Walton takes us back to our starting point, to PESTLE and the importance of understanding context. He explores how leaders must move from vision to success by: linking goals, strategy and action; by empowering teams through skilled job design and professional growth; by mastering efficiency through the analysis of management procedures and systems; by defining success through measuring performance and growth; and by shaping culture through assessing their impact on climate.

He concludes:

> *Educational leadership is not for the faint-hearted. It demands vision, adaptability, and an unwavering commitment to excellence. However, the rewards are profound: empowered and successful students, motivated staff, and organisations that not only meet expectations but exceed them.*

References

Alexander, R. (2000) *Culture and Pedagogy: International Comparisons in Primary Education*. Oxford: Blackwell.

Archer, M. (1984) *Social Origins of Educational Systems*. London: Sage.

Association of Education Advisers (2025) *Senior Associate Seminar*. Newcastle: AoEA.

Beck, M. (2024) *Mobile Phones in School: Mandating a Ban*. UK Parliament, House of Lords Library. Online at: https://lordslibrary.parliament.uk/mobile-phones-in-schools-mandating-a-ban/. (Accessed on 26/02/25).

Crehan, L. (2016) *Cleverlands*. London: Unbound.

Engeström, Y. (1987) *Learning by Expanding: An Activity-Theoretical Approach to Developmental Research*. Helsinki: Orienta-Konsultit.

Hargreaves, A., & Fullan, M. (2012) *Professional Capital: Transforming Teaching in Every School*. New York: Teachers College Press.

Knights, E. (2025) The evolution of governance: Reflections on supporting improvement from 2010 to 2024. In *Advising on Governance in Education*. Association of Education Advisers. London: Routledge.

Leithwood, K., Harris, A., & Hopkins, D. (2019) Seven strong claims about successful school leadership revisited. *School Leadership and Management*, 40(1), 5–22.

MacBeath, J. (1999) *Schools Must Speak for Themselves: The Case for School Self-Evaluation*. London: Routledge.

Simon, J. (1966) *Education and Society in Tudor England*. Cambridge: Cambridge University Press.

Part 1
Advising on organisational development in the context of change

1 Future-proofing your organisation with PESTLE

IAN LANE

Key learning

- No society stands still, and by implication, change for organisations in any country or jurisdiction is both inevitable and continuous.

- Embracing and seeking to understand PESTLE – the political, economic, social, technological, legal and environmental drivers for change – will support leaders in future-proofing their organisations.

- Education advisers have a key role to play in assisting leaders in understanding and interpreting the key drivers for change which impact on their organisations.

- A periodic and systematic evaluation of PESTLE will help to bring a proactive approach to organisational development for the school and for its connection with a wider system of schools; one which seeks to address both immediate needs and longer-term aspirations and goals for all children and young people.

AoEA criteria

- Criterion 21: Understands the PESTLE drivers for change

- Criterion 23: Is able to link vision, policy, strategy, plans, goals and ambitions to long-term requirements and immediate needs

Introduction

This chapter looks at how an education adviser might assist leaders in an analysis of PESTLE as part of a periodic process of review, evaluation and continuous improvement so that leaders are well-placed to anticipate and plan for, rather than react to, change. The purpose underpinning this process is to bring a proactive approach to organisational development – one which assists in delivering to both immediate needs as well as longer-term strategic goals. When an analysis of external drivers impacting on an organisation is undertaken as part of planning, the PESTLE part of the process can often be too hastily undertaken or rushed, yet, when undertaken well, it can provide a powerful means of enabling a shared understanding of the development needs at every level of the organisation. It can help to strengthen a sense of unity and common purpose across leadership teams, whole staff teams, for leaders working with their governors, and for schools working across a wider system of schools. Education advisers are well-placed to support leaders as the architects of an inevitable process of change but one which they lead and manage in accordance with their values as opposed to one which manages them.

Emphasis throughout this chapter, as illustrated in the following diagram (Figure 1.1), will be on exploring those key PESTLE drivers for change and their impact on organisational development.

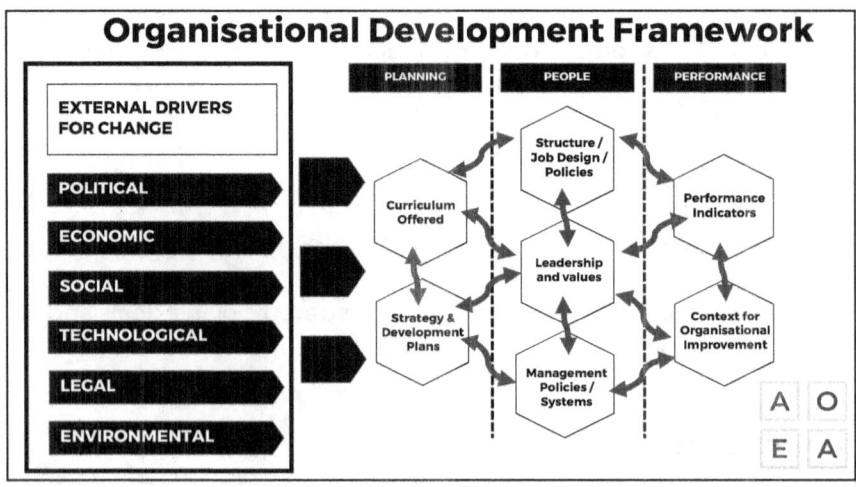

Figure 1.1 The impact of PESTLE on organisational development

Why PESTLE and why a framework for organisational development

PESTLE is integral to the organisational development framework, which helps to provide a holistic view and an objective, strategic lens through which to see the organisation, whether that be for an individual school, a federated group of schools, a regional or local authority – a national system of schools even. Some would argue that for too long, in England, focus has been on trying to address individual elements of an organisational development framework rather than a strategic attempt to link and align the component parts which make up the whole. Curriculum design, for example, needs to reflect the needs of a modern world – its economic, social and technological needs. Teachers need the skills and continuous professional learning to deliver to that need, equipped with the necessary resources, and curriculum and assessment should appropriately ensure the teaching of and measure the knowledge and skills and, ultimately, the performance that we're after. Hence, the linking of planning, people and performance, reflecting those key drivers for change and in all aspects of the school's work.

The organisational development framework, then, identifies the component parts that, when seen together, provide a powerful structure through which to evaluate the operation of the whole organisation. It is a model that sees school improvement as activity that takes place within this holistic context, not simply an intervention that looks at one part of the operation in isolation. Similarly, the framework does not assume that the school improvement process is a linear one beginning with one element, such as a plan, and rolling it out to envelop everything within the whole organisation. This model reflects the complexity of school development and encourages leaders to home in on those areas where they perceive improvement is needed most.

Some of the benefits of the organisational development framework can be summarised as follows:

- It is timeless. It was as relevant 30 years ago as it is now. The technology, for example, may have looked very different, and while at that time, we were not even discussing the intricacies of artificial intelligence, technological advancement was, nevertheless, a key driver for change. The case can be argued similarly in relation to each of the PESTLE drivers as well as for their implications for the component parts of the organisational development framework.

- It provides an objective, strategic lens through which to see the organisation. It can, in a dispassionate way, be used to reinforce focus across a team or a group of schools. It can be used equally effectively to unify a disparate group of key decision-makers.
- It can be applied to any organisation: a school, college, local authority, trust or other federated group of schools. Read 'curriculum offer' as the 'service offered', for example, in an education authority's school improvement service.
- It can be applied to departments within an organisation as well as the organisation as a whole. Priorities in one part of the organisation might be very different from another as a result of, for example, the way that national policy is impacting on each. New curricula can often be phased in, providing more pressing need for one subject department within a school as opposed to another or for one section, for example, of an education authority's work with its schools.
- It can apply equally to organisations based in the UK or internationally. All the component parts are as pertinent.
- It can be a helpful, self-reflective tool. I've often used it in this way to remind me (i) that it is the sands that have shifted and not our values and (ii) that we need to realign and manage the change before it manages us. Similarly, that initial thinking and reflection, leading into a closer analysis of the issues facing the organisation, can be widened to include advisers, leadership teams and groups of schools.
- The framework can also be used to help contextualise a review process or a report. In presenting to governance boards, what is, for example, the current national direction of travel, what are the key implications and what action are we taking to stay ahead of the curve?

- Importantly, it can apply equally to the high-performing school as it does to those facing the most challenge, since the focus is on continuous improvement no matter the starting point.

The PESTLE analysis process

An analysis of the political, economic, social, technological, legal and environmental areas has three main purposes:

1. To identify issues that are outside of the control of the organisation;
2. To identify those which will have some level of impact on the organisation itself;
3. To prioritise in relation to potential development, given where the school, college or provider is currently at in relation to its performance.

The PESTLE analysis process itself needs to be carefully managed to ensure that the focus is on identification and 'teasing out' the issues as opposed to attempting to resolve them or diving too readily into the detail. Discussion at this point may well trigger the need to focus more carefully on specific areas of organisational development. To optimise both the efficiency of this process and any consequent planning and implementation, there is also a need to prioritise those issues most pertinent to the organisation. Figure 1.2 provides a helpful point of reference for this.

The principal aim is to identify the key implications for the school or organisation going forward. A skilful adviser, with an independent eye on things, can assist in its facilitation.

Thought too should be given to those who participate in this process. Involvement of key stakeholders and change agents will strengthen ownership and a collaborative commitment to the organisation's development needs. The adviser will need to take the time with leadership and/or governance to determine who needs to be there to ensure that needs are not only understood but that they are owned and can be acted upon, following this initial process.

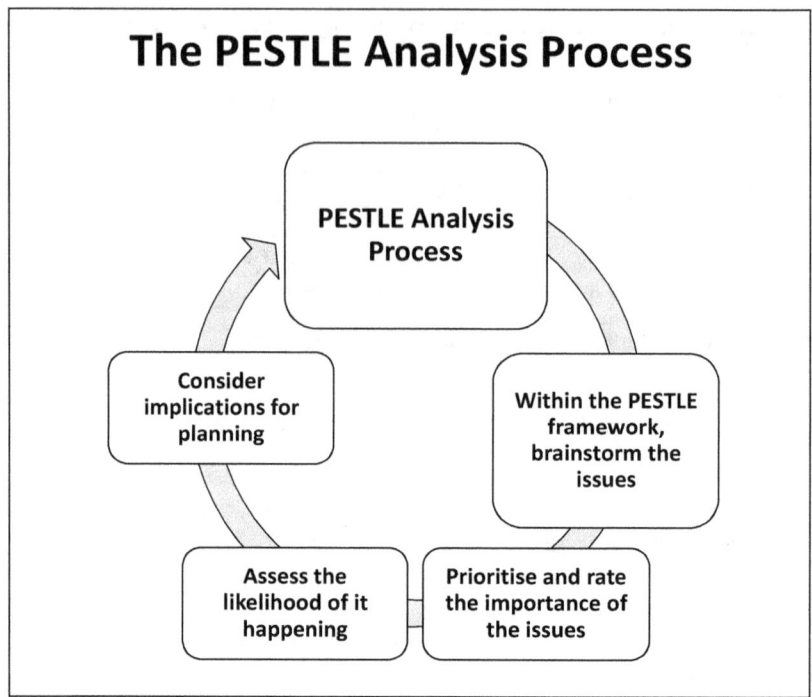

Figure 1.2 PESTLE analysis process

The following case study helps to illustrate how the PESTLE analysis might be applied in enabling leadership and governance, in this case, to have a better understanding of its organisational development needs.

PESTLE case study

Context

This local authority-maintained secondary special school decided to procure the services of an education adviser to support leadership and governance in looking at its planning priorities in the context of change at its annual leadership residential. Although annual review, evaluation and planning were established practice, there was a need to connect leaders, governance and one or two key change agents with some important, wider educational developments. A proposed new White Paper, among other things, was pressing for structural change for all schools in the local authority–maintained sector, to be implemented within 10 years. There was also a proposed new SEND Bill on the horizon. As an outstanding, special school and key player in supporting SEND provision with the local authority, there were also important implications in relation to wider system leadership development going forward.

In consultation with leadership and the school's governance, it was agreed that the organisational development framework would be used as a point of reference, beginning with PESTLE, to assist in determining the key drivers for change faced by the school. This would then provide a helpful lead-in to understanding and embracing some key national drivers for change, undertaking a Strengths, Weaknesses, Opportunities, Threats (SWOT) self-evaluation exercise prior to finally beginning to confirm key priorities for the school's development planning cycle and next steps.

No one was under any illusion that this conference would come up with all the answers, but it would helpfully begin to connect leaders, governors and some key stakeholders in a process of change, and with all on side, or with all at least understanding that there were some key issues to be factored into thinking and strategy.

A visual outline of where the process would lead is illustrated in Figure 1.3.

When working with a relatively large group with varying degrees of delegated authority and views, it is helpful to take the precaution of establishing the ground rules. This was to be:

- a collaborative, team effort;
- one where every individual's contribution was of equal value;
- one where there was no such thing as a 'daft question' or 'daft idea';
- at this stage, completely confidential to the group to 'free everyone up' to think strategically together;

- enjoyable. Fun was a declared, essential ingredient and the conference provided a great opportunity to connect further a wider team of busy people with a common purpose and one which we wanted them to enjoy. We wanted them to rise to the challenge and to want to come back for more!

A key aim, integral to PESTLE, was to ensure that the 'bigger picture' thinking took place, enable interrogation of some key national drivers for change, prior to then considering which ones applied most to the organisation.

The PESTLE rubric was helpful in ensuring an objective analysis of the key issues in the context of change. There was some stimulus to thinking for each PESTLE area supported with some key questions. Some of the most pertinent questions were:

- What is the government's direction of travel and what are the key policy drivers?

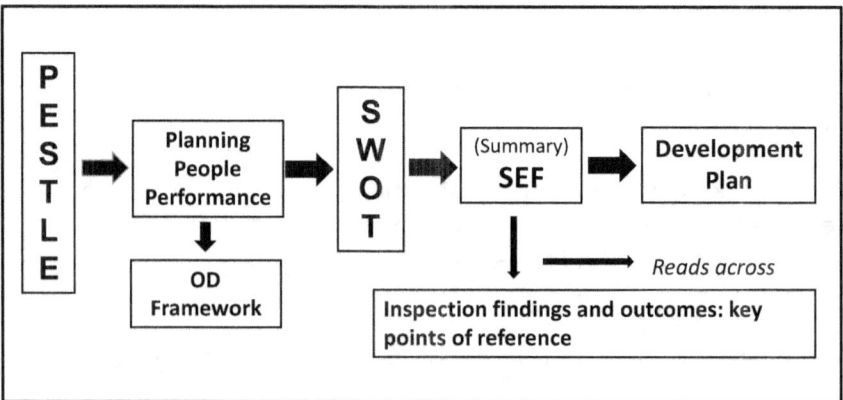

Figure 1.3 PESTLE informed organisational development planning process

- What are the strategic planning issues for governance at school, regional and national levels?
- What is the evolving role of national, regional and local decision-makers?
- Are there opportunities? Are there risks?
- Does the vision for the organisation need re-aligning?
- How do we remain loyal to our values of inclusion and collaboration in this context of a changing education environment?
- In the context of a new regulatory framework, are there areas of our work which need to be even more sharply focused or more explicitly expressed?

Some of the key areas of focus were supported with presentations and the relevant documentation and detail, such as in relation to opportunities and risks associated with structural change.

A number of the issues and resultant actions were identified, including:

- an options appraisal of whether to remain as a local authority–maintained school or to form or to join a multi-academy trust;
- the consideration of whether or not the school's vision and values statements needed re-alignment to ensure that it was still fit for purpose and with a view to better communicating its mission to key national, regional and local stakeholders;
- which organisations to work more closely with or to contact in relation to potential structural change for the school and its part as a wider collaborative of schools;
- consideration of the opportunities for system leadership within a changing education landscape.

In teasing out some of the 'bigger' issues and potential threats, the feeling of coming to grips with the direction of travel and feeling in control also enabled a more energised focus on the 'business as usual' in securing optimum impact on outcomes.

Having considered the impact of PESTLE on the organisation's planning, people and performance, a SWOT analysis was undertaken in each of the areas of the school's provision to better understand the school's current strengths and needs for the coming and subsequent years.

This seamlessly led into a succinct revision of the school's self-evaluation and towards a more careful consideration of what needed to be included in the school's strategic development plan.

Impact of this process

- Enablement of objectivity and collaborative analysis in relation to some key external drivers for change, one or two of which had been hitherto emotionally charged and of concern to key stakeholders.

- Leadership and governance having a better informed and shared understanding of the wider educational landscape and how the organisation needed to 'future-proof' itself and maximise opportunities in the best interests of its young people, without compromising on any of its core principles and values.

- A more objective understanding of the school's performance within both a national and local context with an eye on its own needs for further, sustained improvement as an outstanding school, as well as how it might contribute more significantly to the greater good in collaboration with others.

- A more succinct and better-informed summary self-evaluation form in all areas of provision, informed by key external drivers and the school's own strengths and areas for further development.

- A school development plan which followed and provided a clear roadmap for the school and for the purposes of informing accountability and to which all key stakeholders had constructively contributed.

- Leadership and governance feeling more in control of its own destiny as a manager of change as opposed to being a mere recipient of it.

Conclusion

Many of the challenges that schools and their providers face are generated from outside the organisation by national, regional or local direction of travel. These can range from change in national policy to broader environmental factors in which the schools operate or legacy issues of underperformance impacting on local, negative perception, for example, that may take years to shift. Schools and education providers can be drawn into addressing needs on an individual basis or by policy that demands results 'overnight'. By using a well-structured PESTLE analysis, advisers working with their schools, providers and key stakeholders can assess the nature of the challenges that they face and make a more considered assessment of the scale of the impact each one may have on the organisation. It is a process that is both enabling and empowering for leaders in affecting their own organisational effectiveness in the context of change and in sustaining the drive to continuously improve the education provision and outcomes for all children and young people.

Further reading

CIPD. *PESTLE Analysis Fact Sheet*. Online at: https://www.cipd.org/uk/knowledge/factsheets/pestle-analysis-factsheet. (Accessed on 31/01/25)

RapidBI. *PESTLE Analysis for Schools or Education*. Online at: PESTLE analysis for schools or education. (Accessed on 31/01/25).

2 Responding to and working with political change: The art of the possible

SIR PETER LAUENER CB

Key learning

- Politics and political decisions have a significant impact on the environment within which schools operate, and therefore on the expectations that parents have, on what curriculum should be provided and on how schools should be held to account for their performance.

- Education advisers need to understand the political context and how that might affect schools and also, on occasion, advise school leaders on how to influence the political environment.

AoEA criteria

- Criterion 21: Understands the PESTLE drivers for change

- Criterion 23: Is able to link policy, strategy, plans and ambitions to long-term requirements and immediate needs

Introduction

This chapter reviews the impact of politics on education in England. Politics is often described as the art of the possible, an aphorism that might equally apply to the role of an education adviser! Politics certainly has an impact on education, at both a national and local level. This chapter sets out the context to this and gives some non-education examples of the power of politics to transform society. It then outlines some landmark education (and training) policy changes, giving examples of legislation, funding and the power of ideas, even without legislation. Three examples from the last 30 years are then set out in terms of the principles of change that were being applied and, therefore, on the national framework of objectives within which all schools operate. This leads to some suggested pointers for school leaders and education advisers as they chart their own path through political change.

The power of political change to transform society

A great starting point is to think of some of the significant changes made in society through the power of Parliament to change the laws which govern how society works.

Here are some of my own favourite 'great society changes' enabled by political change:

- The Abolition of Slavery Act of 1833;
- The gradual extension of voting rights, especially the (eventual) response to the suffragette movement in the UK with the extension to all women of voting rights in 1928. Many countries beat the UK to this landmark;
- The Clean Air Act of 1956, which has forever done away with the 'smogs', which could last for days on end in the 1950s and 1960s and which older readers will remember;
- The legalisation of homosexual activity through the Sexual Offences Act of 1967 (famously managed through Parliament through a private member's bill by a very young David Steel, albeit with the blessing of the Home Secretary, Roy Jenkins); and
- The Health and Safety at Work Act of 1974, which has saved many lives; in construction the number of site deaths has fallen by 90% in the last 50 years.

This is my own choice of some landmark political changes. What would be on your own list, and what would young people today want to change for the future?

Bringing it back to education, let me give some examples where political action has changed the way we educate our children and young people. Let me start again with some important pieces of legislation. Politics can affect what happens in any or all of three ways, through:

- legislation;
- persuasion and debate;
- money.

My personal favourite piece of legislation relevant to education and training is an Act called the Statute of Artificers, which parliament passed in 1563. It covered aspects such as the trades that young men (yes, they were all male) could be apprenticed in, the number of apprentices any master could employ (no more than three) and how long apprenticeships lasted (seven years). Interesting, isn't it, that this was passed some 300 years before the first legislation about school education!

And, of course, that is because for hundreds of years, education was not seen as the business of the state but of parents who could afford private tutors and of charities or the church, which were socially motivated to provide education to the poor in society.

But this resulted in a patchwork provision of education and the first comprehensive Act covering schools was the Elementary Education Act of 1870, which divided England into districts under the management of locally elected school boards. In effect, these board schools were the first schools run by local authorities. My own grandfather in Scotland ran such a school on a remote island in the Western Isles, and one of his responsibilities was to keep a regular written log of activities which I was able recently to read, a hundred years after he wrote it, in a local archive. It conveyed rather graphically the need to satisfy the school inspector who would descend from time to time from the local education board to visit the school and make sure that funding was being properly used!

Other important pieces of legislation which readers will be very familiar with include:

- The Butler Education Act of 1944, which established a tripartite system of categories of school: grammar, secondary modern and technical. The Act also raised the school leaving age to 15 and set an expectation (not implemented until 1972) that it would be raised in due course to 16. Note that successive governments have failed to make the funding available to provide sufficient technical education;

- The 1976 Education Act, which established 'the comprehensive principle' which led to the requirement for local authorities to bring forward proposals for the reorganisation of local schools;
- The 1988 Education Reform Act saw the establishment of the National Curriculum, a major step towards the centralisation of education policy, which also led to the creation of grant-maintained schools, leading 20 years later to the development of the academy movement;
- The Learning and Skills Act 2000 which both established the framework for academies and repealed Section 28, which had outlawed the promotion of homosexuality as well as its primary purpose of establishing the Learning and Skills Council for post-16 education and training.

But remember, politics is not just about legislation. It includes the power of persuasion and the power to spend money voted by Parliament. Some more examples:

- The development of Mechanics' Institutes as the Industrial Revolution changed the face of society. These were established by local industrialists and civic leaders, both to develop the skills needed by rapidly expanding industry and to provide more socially useful activities than the local public house! They are perhaps the best example of a movement developing without government funding. The first was established in 1821 in Edinburgh at what is now Heriot Watt University and within 40 years, there were over 700 examples in almost every town or city in the country.
- Jim Callaghan's Ruskin College speech of 1976, which is widely seen as beginning a great debate about the nature and purpose of public education. Callaghan has often been portrayed as calling for a bigger focus on the 3 Rs (reading, writing and arithmetic). But it was much more than that, and I still find it an inspirational speech. At its heart, it was about developing a system which will allow all children to fulfil their potential, earn a good living, supporting a productive economy and be constructive members of their local community.

- My last example is the Manpower Services Commission, established very simply to make arrangements for employment and training under the Employment and Training Act 1974 but achieving some significant changes in society and addressing the impacts of high unemployment in the 1980s through imaginative and creative tripartite programmes, with substantial flexibility over programme design and the funding to act quickly. It also fostered more acronyms than any other organisation at the time so how many of the following can you spell out (answers at the end!): YOP, CP, WEEP, TVEI, EHE, YTS, JCP, JTS.

Developing a framework of national objectives

Every education adviser will expect to see a clear framework of objectives for any school when they are called in to advise on how it should develop. So, how does this framework compare at national level?

Let us compare examples from three secretaries of state. Here are David Blunkett's principles for the education system set out in his White Paper 'Excellence in Schools', published just two months after the May 1997 general election:

1. Education will be at the heart of government.
2. Policies will be designed to benefit the many, not just the few.
3. The focus will be on standards, not structures.
4. Intervention will be in inverse proportion to success.
5. There will be zero tolerance of underperformance.
6. Government will work in partnership with all those committed to raising standards.

And here, for comparison, are Michael Gove's principles, set out rather later in his tenure as secretary of state in a speech he gave in June 2014:

1. There will be maximum autonomy for a school headteacher.
2. There will be rigorous accountability for performance.

3. There will be high-quality teaching.
4. There will be strict behaviour policies.
5. There will be an ambitious curriculum with a particular focus on core subjects to age 16.

There is one other framework of principles which is worth highlighting as an example of cross-government activity, led by Ed Balls when he was secretary of state for Children, schools and families. Produced some 20 years ago, the *Every Child Matters* Framework still resonates strongly with professional colleagues working in education, health and social care. This approach was supported by the Children's Act 2004 and set an overall set of goals that irrespective of social background or individual circumstances, every child should:

- be healthy;
- stay safe;
- enjoy and achieve;
- make a positive contribution;
- achieve economic well-being.

Each objective had its own detailed set of measures, requiring multi-agency partnerships to deliver success. And, areas of focus included youth justice; education, training and employment; parents, carers and families; early years and child care; culture, sport and play; children's and young people's health; youth matters; and social care, welfare and protection.

You will see different words used in these principles and frameworks, and they also convey a different tone and context in policy, which in all three cases resulted in a shift in the way schools needed to respond.

To illustrate:

- David Blunkett's principles led to a huge focus on standards in primary schools during the 1997–2001 Labour Government, with a drive from the literacy and numeracy hours, which successfully raised standards with additional support from education advisers for any school seen to be 'behind the curve' on standards.

- Michael Gove's approach was designed to develop a school-led system with good and outstanding schools converting to academies and leading other schools which were less successful.
- Ed Balls focused on the needs of the whole child, on the basis that an unhealthy child or a child without good care would not be able to learn well. To my mind, there are shades in *Every Child Matters* of Jim Callaghan's Ruskin College speech.

So there were clear differences in philosophy in these three approaches, but what these three secretaries of state had in common was an unrelenting focus on making a difference and driving progress in improving outcomes for our children. They were all demanding of their civil servants and always impatient with the pace of reform. In my experience, that kind of political drive and passion is an essential requirement to affect change at local as much as at national level.

Conclusion

Implications for education advisers supporting schools

My examples of education policy are all at national level because that is what I saw day to day in my career. But I also had considerable contact with local authority leaders and saw many examples where local change was both enabled and driven by an effective lead member for children's services and the executive director with that brief. The general lessons I draw for the role of education advisers in supporting schools are:

- Understand the key drivers in national education policy and discuss with any school you are supporting how they are responding to national policy drivers. It may be that leaders in a particular school do not agree with a particular policy, but you should question whether that is for good reasons or bad – and whether a school is achieving acceptable standards by other means.
- Establish whether a school you are supporting has strong engagement with local MPs and local ward councillors, who can be helpful in dealing with local difficult issues where the school needs help such as access to support services. Is the school part of its community and serving its community or does it seem insular and unaware of its role beyond education?

- Using both the *Every Child Matters* framework and the focus of the Ruskin College speech, is the school focused sufficiently on how it can help its pupils become confident, assured adults with the potential to earn a good living and contribute to their communities?

Some might say that takes a school too far from its fundamental purpose of education. I disagree. A happy child will learn better. A healthy child will learn better. A child with a loving family and good care will learn better. Whether in England or any other jurisdiction, the same applies.

Further reading

Gove, M. (7 June 2014) *The Purpose of Our School Reforms*. Government Policy Exchange. Online at: https://www.gov.uk/government/speeches/the-purpose-of-our-school-reforms. (Accessed on 06/05/25).

Training Services, Manpower Services Commission (1981) *Glossary of Training Terms*. London: Department of Employment.

Answers to the 'name that scheme' challenge

YOP: Youth Opportunities Programme

CP: Community Programme

WEEP: Work Experience on Employer's Premises

TVEI: Technical and Vocational Education Initiative

EHE: Enterprise in Higher Education

YTS: Youth Training Scheme

JCP: Job Creation Programme

JTS: Job Training Scheme

3 Advising on organisational development in a fast-changing technological context

AL KINGSLEY MBE

Key learning

- We create clarity by articulating why change is needed and how it aligns with our mission.

- We move forward by ensuring staff feel valued, prepared and supported in their professional growth.

- We remain open to new technologies, but we scrutinise them through the lens of impact, equity and sustainability.

- We cultivate a culture of reflection and collaboration, so our organisations learn from both successes and missteps.

AoEA criteria

- Criterion 21: Understands the PESTLE drivers for change

- Criterion 22: Critically evaluates the design of the curriculum or educational offer

- Criterion 23: Is able to link vision, policy, strategy, plans, goals and ambitions to long-term requirements and immediate needs

- Criterion 24: Links the job design and people development to strategic requirements

- Criterion 25: Is able to analyse management procedures and systems

- Criterion 26: Is able to apply a variety of measurements of success and performance indicators

- Criterion 27: Is able to assess the context for organisational improvement

Introduction

In an era where the pace of technological change shows no sign of slowing, educational organisations, particularly those working within the English school system, must be prepared to adapt swiftly and strategically. Many of us in education leadership, governance, or advisory capacities have already seen how an ability to navigate change can determine whether schools thrive or falter in uncertain times. In my previous books, I have often stressed the importance of approaching organisational development from both a broad strategic lens and the smallest practical details that affect our students, staff, and communities daily. This chapter will draw on themes, guidance, and discussions from *My School Governance Handbook* (2022), *MAT Growth Handbook* (2023), and *The Awkward Questions in Education* (2025) to provide an integrated view of how, where appropriate, advisers can support leadership teams to harness technology and digital tools effectively, manage strategic growth, and safeguard the ethos and values that underscore the English education context.

Setting the scene: the changing landscape

Across the education sector in England, the operating environment has shifted considerably over recent years. From policy reforms and funding pressures to the rise in multi-academy trusts (MATs) and academisation, leaders must not only handle existing demands but anticipate those that are still on the horizon. Then we add in technological innovations, particularly in areas such as artificial intelligence (AI), online learning, and digital communication tools, and the rate of change intensifies further.

In *The Awkward Questions in Education*, I explore how new technologies, including AI, are knocking at the doors of our classrooms, posing opportunities and challenges for everyone involved – leaders, teachers, parents, and students alike. While AI might present game-changing prospects for personalised learning and automating certain tasks, it also raises legitimate concerns around data privacy, student well-being, digital equity, and the preparedness of staff to integrate these tools responsibly. It is in that tension, between excitement and caution, that organisational development must find its anchor: leading with a clear moral purpose, a commitment to inclusivity, and strategic oversight that ensures technology truly serves our educational aims rather than dictating them.

Organisational development: a foundation for change

Organisational development (OD) is, at its heart, a systematic process for planning and implementing change in order to align structure, process, and culture with organisational goals. Within English education, this involves the interplay of governance, leadership, and the day-to-day experience in schools. The idea of 'shared purpose' is often emphasised in education, yet it can only remain meaningful if the entire organisation – trustees, governors, executive leaders, and staff – has clarity on the direction and rationale behind strategic changes.

In *My School Governance Handbook*, I describe how robust governance creates the space for that clarity. A strong board ensures that strategic decisions about school improvement, collaboration with external partners, and the adoption of technology are scrutinised with children's outcomes and well-being front and centre. Indeed, I continue to argue in a broader sense that one of the biggest challenges for governors is not only understanding the pace of innovation but also ensuring it aligns with the school's overall mission and values. When boards actively participate in self-assessment, anticipate risks, and identify opportunities, they become a powerful force to steer organisational development. Conversely, when governance is left to reactive oversight, much of the potential for coherent change is lost.

In practical terms, good OD demands the following baseline elements:
- *A clear, ambitious vision*. Leadership should articulate what success looks like for the organisation in three, five, and ten years' time. This vision goes beyond league table positions. It might focus on how technology can foster creativity or how the curriculum supports our learners in thriving in a changing world.

- *Collaborative culture*. As emphasised in *The Awkward Questions in Education*, schools cannot innovate in silos. Collaboration is pivotal, whether between senior leaders, classroom practitioners, the wider community, or external partners, so that fresh ideas and best practices feed into strategic goals.
- *Capacity and skill-building*. To deliver sustainable change, staff at all levels need ongoing professional learning, especially around digital tools. As I noted,

> - *Staff needs to be given resources and time to develop their own competencies and confidence, ideally as part of their teacher training from now on, and we must empower our students to be the best possible digital citizens, which will go a long way to equipping them for an AI-driven workplace.*
>
> (Kingsley, 2025, p. 118)

Digital as a lever for change

When it comes to using technology and digital platforms as a lever for organisational adaptation, the principle to remember is that technology is an enabler, not an end in itself. In my *MAT Growth Handbook*, I reflected on how digital innovations must be integrated with clarity of purpose. A commonly overlooked danger is adopting new technologies without adequately exploring whether they truly serve a strategic objective or whether they introduce unintended workload burdens on staff.

Aligning digital strategy with organisational goals

Before rolling out new devices, software platforms, or AI-driven tools, senior leaders should define what they want to accomplish. Are you aiming to improve student engagement through more personalised approaches? Is the focus on staff efficiency, perhaps by automating administrative tasks so teachers can devote more time to high-quality teaching and learning? Are you seeking better channels to engage parents or to expand the school's presence in the wider community? Whatever the objective, clarity on the 'why' makes it far easier to evaluate whether a technology solution is suitable. Digital strategy, in that sense, becomes part of the overall organisational development plan, fostering coherence and preventing the 'tech for tech's sake' phenomenon.

Building staff confidence and competencies

The most powerful digital transformation initiatives often falter because of staff anxiety, skill gaps, or a simple lack of time for training. Especially in large MATs, variation in skill sets can be pronounced. In *My School Governance Handbook*, I stress the importance of governors and trustees asking incisive questions about professional development that feed into thinking about topics such as:

- How is staff voice incorporated into the selection of digital tools?
- Do leaders provide a phased rollout with appropriate training and peer support?
- Are staff given time to embed these tools into their practice, or is this another 'bolt-on' to an already busy schedule?

When staff are engaged and see technology as supportive – not an extra burden – it can radically alter the school's capacity to innovate and respond to challenges, such as remote learning during closures or the need for flexible provision to cope with varied student attendance patterns.

Developing digital citizenship and safeguarding

Organisational development in the digital space isn't just about staff skills or strategic alignment; it also concerns students' development into informed, responsible digital citizens. As I have suggested many times across my publications, that schools must embed e-safety, digital literacy, and awareness of online risks into their strategic planning; for example, adopting a wide range of online applications for learning must be complemented by robust data protection processes, staff training in safeguarding protocols, and continuous dialogue with parents about online risks. Students must learn not only how to use digital tools but also how to engage with technology and AI ethically and responsibly.

In the context of a fast-changing landscape, leaders must keep one eye on emerging trends, such as the rise of generative AI in education, whilst simultaneously reviewing whether adequate policies and support structures are in place to protect young people's well-being. This dual focus is another hallmark of healthy organisational development – being progressive yet responsible in technology adoption.

Growth, collaboration, and the MAT model

A core theme in organisational development within the English system is the growth and collaboration facilitated by multi-academy trusts (MATs). The MAT model offers the potential for economies of scale, shared resources, and cross-pollination of ideas; essential ingredients for thriving in a dynamic environment. However, growth for growth's sake can also strain resources if not undertaken carefully. I always try and set out that strategic growth involves:

- *Due diligence.* Thoroughly understanding prospective schools' contexts, finances, and local challenges before bringing them into the trust. Leadership teams that skip this step risk inheriting unsustainable cost bases or cultures misaligned with the trust's core ethos.
- *Clear vision for collaboration.* A successful MAT fosters knowledge-sharing, joint professional learning opportunities, and unified approaches to technology. Without intentional collaboration structures, such as cross-trust working groups or platforms for teacher exchanges, any synergy from growth is left purely to chance.
- *Governance capacity.* With each additional school, new governance challenges arise. Trustees must consider whether their board has the expertise, bandwidth, and diversity needed to oversee multiple schools operating at different performance and maturity levels. The principle of '*if you grow, ensure your governance grows too*' has been a consistent refrain in for some years.

Importantly, fast-paced technology changes and a growing trust can intersect. For example, as trusts expand, they may roll out digital platforms across a wider network. That scale brings advantages: central procurement cost savings, a shared best-practice library, and consistent data systems for monitoring progress. Yet with scale also comes the challenge of ensuring equitable access and consistent digital infrastructures. Remote rural schools may need more robust connectivity solutions than their urban counterparts, for instance, and the MAT's organisational strategy must address those variations with empathy and foresight.

Ensuring long-term sustainability

Short-term improvements – better attendance data, higher exam results, or a successful rollout of an edtech platform are welcome, but organisational development should always be anchored in long-term thinking. Sustainability here spans financial stability, staff well-being, and the capacity of the organisation to keep innovating as circumstances inevitably evolve.

Financial stewardship

In *My School Governance Handbook*, I highlight that *'good governance includes understanding the budget well enough to ask the right questions'* (Kingsley, 2022, p. 69). Leaders must anticipate technology's total cost of ownership (licences, device refresh cycles, staff training, technical support) and weigh it against real-world impact on educational outcomes. Some changes that appear beneficial in the short-term might carry hidden costs that undermine an institution's financial position.

Well-being for staff and learners

As the pace of change accelerates, spurred by technology, shifting examination criteria, and new collaborative structures, staff often feel the strain. Any OD plan that fails to address workload, mental health support, and professional autonomy risks a high attrition rate and plummeting morale. The best leadership teams embed well-being measures into every phase of their strategic planning, whether that's refining marking policies through technology to reduce teacher workload or scheduling mandatory 'downtime' from emails to prevent burnout.

Continuous improvement mindset

No organisational development plan, however well-conceived, remains perfect forever. Especially in a fast-changing technological environment, it is vital that schools and trusts institute a culture of iterative improvement. Regularly conducted 'health checks' of digital initiatives, staff feedback sessions, and pilot programmes before major rollouts can all help refine an approach early on. In *The Awkward Questions in Education*, I argue that genuine self-reflection, backed by data and stakeholder engagement, helps identify both blind spots and new opportunities for improvement.

Leadership and governance: guiding the journey

A recurring theme across all my writing is that strong governance and leadership are the 'guardrails' for effective organisational development. While the speed of technology change can feel daunting, a resilient leadership team, supported by an informed and cohesive governing board, can turn potential chaos into purposeful innovation.

Governors and trustees, in particular, serve as the strategic conscience of the organisation. They must balance an ambitious vision for improvement with a rigorous understanding of the institution's capacity: its finances, staff skill levels, local community context, and existing obligations. Meanwhile, executive leaders orchestrate daily operations, champion staff development, and translate board-level goals into tangible action.

In many of my discussions, and in each of my books, I highlight the power of asking the right questions. Examples might include:

- *On vision*. How does this proposed technology solution align with our broader educational aims?
- *On capacity*. Have we planned enough training and time for staff to absorb new processes, or are we underestimating the workload?
- *On evidence*. Which measures will tell us if this innovation is genuinely raising attainment or improving well-being?

- *On collaboration.* Are we engaging with other schools, or across our MAT, to share best practice and avoid duplicating effort?

These questions move leaders out of reactive mode and help sustain a future-focused, evidence-informed approach to change.

Maintaining ethos and values through change

A concern often raised when discussing rapid technology adoption or organisational expansion is the fear of losing the distinctive ethos or values that made a school community special in the first place. Indeed, many educators and parents fear an overly mechanistic approach, where test results overshadow creative thinking or digital efficiency outruns personal connection.

Yet, technology itself can be harnessed to reinforce ethos. Schools might use platforms to celebrate student achievements online or share community-building stories. MATs can organise trust-wide virtual assemblies that underline a collective culture. Systems can be introduced for early detection of pastoral concerns, giving staff more time to focus on timely interventions and forging deeper connections with pupils. In that sense, digital can be a powerful amplifier of a school's values if integrated mindfully.

On a strategic level, the board's responsibility is to ensure that every proposed development, whether structural or technological, is tested against the shared values. This includes evaluating whether, for instance, adopting AI-based learning platforms inadvertently devalues the essential role of the teacher or whether a hasty expansion might jeopardise the quality of pastoral care in existing schools. The motto remains: '*we adapt, but we do not lose sight of who we are*'.

Conclusion

In the rapidly evolving landscape of English education, organisational development must keep one eye firmly on the future while safeguarding the enduring qualities of great teaching and learning. No matter how advanced our technologies become, or how large our

MATs grow, the ultimate test of any change is whether it advances the interests and well-being of children. When leadership, governance, and staff share that North Star, 'fast-changing' environments become not threats but opportunities to renew and refine our practice.

- We create clarity by articulating why change is needed and how it aligns with our mission.
- We move forward by ensuring staff feel valued, prepared, and supported in their professional growth.
- We remain open to new technologies, but we scrutinise them through the lens of impact, equity, and sustainability.
- We cultivate a culture of reflection and collaboration, so our organisations learn from both successes and missteps.

As I have found throughout my own journey, whether in advising MATs, writing about governance, or exploring the awkward questions in education, the key is balance. We embrace innovation without being dazzled by it. We foster growth but do so responsibly. We aim high for the good of each child, yet we remain realistic about capacity and resources. With effective leadership, joined-up governance, and a commitment to the ethos that defines us, English schools can do more than keep up with the times, they can truly thrive in them.

I would always argue, that rather than referring to floor targets and Ofsted inspection grades as the only measure of organisational success, children need us to be talking about how schools develop enterprise, how we can enable them to access opportunities to learn a wide range of languages and understand and engage with other cultures – and how we ensure that children are empowered masters of technology.

This, for me, captures the essence of organisational development in a fast-changing technological context. We expand our horizons, we remain mindful of the moral and cultural dimensions of education and we strive to place digital innovation at the service of a higher goal: helping every learner flourish in a complex and rapidly shifting world. By weaving together strategic intent, good governance, dedicated leadership, and careful implementation of technology, we can strengthen our schools today and prepare them for the uncertainties of tomorrow.

References

Kingsley, A. (2022) *My School Governance Handbook*. United Kingdom: John Catt Educational.

Kingsley, A. (2023) *MAT Growth Handbook*. United Kingdom: John Catt Educational.

Kingsley, A. (2025) *The Awkward Questions in Education*. United Kingdom: Routledge.

Note: All publications referenced are by the same author and reflect guidance and insights on organisational development, governance, and managing change within the English education landscape.

4 Managing the risks of structural change

JOANNE DAVISON

Key learning

- 'Structural change' covers a range of scenarios but there are common themes of which advisers should be aware to help mitigate risk.

- Supporting senior leaders to take the time to prepare, understand and have any challenging discussions is key to success.

- Valued advisers should provide support through ensuring proper preparation, sustaining open communication, asking the right questions, challenging rationale and reminding leaders of the values and ethos that are guiding the change.

AoEA criteria

- Criterion 23: Is able to link vision, policy, strategy, plans, goals and ambitions to long-term requirements and immediate needs

- Criterion 24: Links the job design and people development to strategic requirements

- Criterion 25: Is able to analyse management procedures and systems

- Criterion 27: Is able to assess the context for organisational improvement

Introduction

As a partner in a nationally recognised education team, I have personally led on hundreds of academy conversions, re-brokerage, transfers and merger projects in the education sector. These range from the conversion of a single primary school to academy status, through to the creation of some of the largest academy trusts in England through merger and growth.

While every project is different, there are common themes which arise in advising in relation to projects resulting in any form of structural change. Being aware of these themes helps advisers guide leaders through the change process.

This chapter is intended to highlight the key areas that advisers may need to have in mind when supporting leaders in approaching structural change in the education sector.

The risks of structural change

Change is the only constant in the education sector, and leaders in education are used to the challenge of navigating change. However, structural change is different to that of curriculum planning, legislative and policy changes. Structural change can be difficult to assess, may not be embarked on voluntarily, can be outside the normal course of operations and is often a new area for leaders to grapple with.

Structural change can come about for a variety of reasons. The most common is through a voluntary change in legal structure, for example, moving from a locally funded–maintained school to centrally funded academy, transfer from the ownership of one trust to another or full-scale merger of entities. However, sometimes change can be forced upon a school which has additional implications for the areas covered by this chapter. This can be, though not exclusively, due to such things as financial challenges brought on by falling student numbers resulting in lack of viability or in the perceived failure in the quality of education being delivered.

As with any project, preparation is key to managing risk, and as advisers, the ability to have an external perspective and a view of the bigger picture is invaluable.

The risks of structural change are summarised in subsequent paragraphs.

Lack of knowledge

Due diligence is key to managing risk with any structural change. Understanding fully what is proposed, the issues that need to be addressed, as well as appreciating the many implications in full, is imperative. This can only be achieved through asking the right questions and gaining an in-depth understanding of the information provided. The level of due diligence that is required on a specific project will depend on the circumstances, but this process should not be underestimated: it needs to be properly planned with the necessary time and resources allocated to it. The outcomes of due diligence, a process frequently commissioned externally, need to be fully understood by school leaders. Often the results of due diligence identify patterns or risk areas which need to be properly managed, allowing leaders to fully assess the risks that will arise when the proposed change has been put into effect. Early identification and mitigation of risks are key.

Implications of change

Before any structural change is contemplated leaders will need to ascertain if they have sufficient resources and expertise internally to facilitate the change. The need for external support should be clarified and, where necessary, put in place. If the structural change is transformational or large scale, it is key that the full implications of the change itself are considered. Are policies and processes still fit for purpose? Does governance need to be strengthened/adapted? These considerations inevitably impact on timescales for successful completion of the project.

Lack of direction

Clarity of purpose for embarking on the project is of paramount importance. Trust boards or governors should be clear as to the reason of pursuing the project, the benefits to their students of progressing, any weaknesses that will be addressed and the risk areas which might result in any decision not to proceed. This will help leaders focus on what they are trying to achieve and ensure discussions and subsequent actions are tailored accordingly. Advisers should provide challenge to ensure the strategic vision is set and cascaded down to people involved and that the level of acceptable risk has been agreed upon.

Lack of communication

With every structural change, it is important that all stakeholders are engaged from an early stage and 'brought on the journey'. It is often about 'winning hearts and minds', and this is often achieved through a well-orchestrated communication strategy and plan. Leaders who misjudge the tone or frequency of this communication will have an uphill struggle in making the change in structure a smooth one. School leaders are ordinarily best placed to develop a communication strategy with their stakeholders since this will be dependent on the context of the school, but care should be taken that key messaging is consistent and clear.

In the case of a merger, communication between the merger parties throughout the project is essential. An adviser can add enormous value here by acting as a neutral party to try and steer discussions and pose necessary questions.

People

At the heart of every educational establishment is its people, inclusive of the students and parents/carers the school serves or the staff they engage. It is, therefore, fitting that at the heart of any structural change is consideration and involvement of its people. While staff are often protected in a merger scenario, employee relations need to be managed carefully. Although structural change can often bring advantages, for example, increased opportunities and peer to peer support, people may understandably be cautious. Any people-related strategy regarding structural change includes making those difficult decisions and handling them appropriately. In a merger situation, a school trust may not need, for example, two executive leadership teams, so there is the need for decisive, though carefully and sensitively managed, change. While leaders can often put off having those tricky conversations, clarity from an early stage is invaluable.

As advisers, it is important to challenge leaders to consider the people implications of a proposed change and encourage early discussions to take place. I have worked on projects where those decisions are made early, and while this did add to the time investment needed in the initial stages, the project went much more smoothly and people felt valued and clear on their role. At the other end of the spectrum, I have worked alongside leadership teams who have delayed having those difficult conversations at the leadership level (both executive and governance). This has resulted in the project timeframe being put at risk, projects coming to an end or discussions having to be undertaken in short order. It often feels as if outcomes are forced in this scenario, which can be counter-productive when trying to foster a positive culture within a new structure.

Failure to make those difficult decisions

In the event of a significant structural change, a number of decisions will have to be made. This can be anything from key staffing changes, change of finance management systems or payroll providers to having to undertake a governance review or significant curriculum delivery changes. At the heart of all these changes is a series of decisions having to be made by leaders. Clarity of strategic direction from governors/trust board alongside a clarity of vision and values assists the leadership team with this, but, fundamentally, operational delivery and the decisions relating to the same rests with the leadership team. While it is not for advisers to make these decisions, leaders should be encouraged to act in a timely manner and in an open and transparent way. Often issues arise with structural change when difficult decisions are made too late in the process or without reasonable justification. For example, in a merger scenario, there may be two different HR and payroll providers. Both may be actively engaged in the project, and the leaders may not want to tackle the decision as to which provider would continue. If this, for example, were to result in a change in payroll provider at a late stage, as frequently happens, this can put unnecessary pressure on finance teams to implement large-scale change within too tight a timeframe. Early planning and well-managed implementation are essential for successful integration of teams and smooth running within a new structure.

Conclusion

There are many risks arising from structural change. However, many of these can be managed by following key principles of preparation, communication and decisive implementation. When a leader is in the midst of a project resulting in structural change, an adviser can be, and should be, invaluable in asking the right questions, helping leaders assess the issues, reminding leaders of the bigger picture and equipping the leader with the tools to navigate their way through what can be a myriad of issues and processes. In my experience, leaders going through a period of structural change can feel isolated and overwhelmed at particular points and having an external adviser who can provide support and challenge as and when required can be key.

5 Beyond comfort zones: Advising on organisational development in turbulent times

CATHERINE REDGRAVE

Key learning

- There are times when advisers are faced with challenges that involve working beyond their comfort zone, requiring humility and a desire for personal growth in knowledge and understanding. Advisers draw on expertise and knowledge available and, in doing so, widen their perspective and model professional learning to others.

- Organisational development and change at scale requires building a careful coalition built on strong reciprocal trust and relationships but embracing the need for challenge and transparency. Advisers need to have a confident voice and also listen carefully and respond tactfully.

- In the initial stages of change, data points are unlikely to show dramatic improvement given the nature of the challenges involved. Nonetheless, meaningful change means working for the long term with an eye for quick successes and careful interpretation of data that can sustain motivation.

- Ambitious change can spread if the focus is clear and the need for improvement accepted. The adviser plays a key role in spreading such influence across the system.

AoEA criteria

- Criterion 21: Understands the PESTLE drivers for change
- Criterion 23: Is able to link vision, mission, policy, strategy, resources, plans, goals and ambitions to long-term requirements and immediate needs
- Criterion 26: Is able to apply a variety of measurements of success and performance indicators
- Criterion 27: Is able to assess the context for organisational improvement

Introduction

The summer of 2020 is a time that many educational professionals will recall. There were two world events that meant schools needed to respond, sometimes daily, to the political, economic, social, technological, legal and environmental (PESTLE) demands that were being placed upon them, challenging core beliefs and changing practice: the pandemic and the murder of George Floyd.

In this chapter, I will explain how the murder of George Floyd was a catalyst in the development of understanding and practice within a local school system that is predominantly 'White British'. It required me to step out of my typical day-to-day school improvement work and, instead, into a space where I felt uncomfortable and ill-equipped on a personal level.

Following the murder of George Floyd and the subsequent protests, rallies and the 'take the knee' show of support, I was made aware of a review into the lived experience of black and minority ethnic (BAME) communities in Basingstoke, Hampshire. The inquiry, publicised through local news and social media, received submissions from individual residents and community groups.

Feedback highlighted issues in workplaces, schools, the community, policing and health. The personal experiences of the local education system revealed some disturbing perceptions, suggesting that schools were:

- often weak in handling racist abuse and dismissive of verbal comments;
- making stereotypical assumptions about pupils' capabilities and setting lower expectations for BAME students;
- focusing the teaching of black history on slavery and under-representing positive contributions by black people;
- employing a workforce that significantly under-represented BAME communities.

As the lead educational adviser responsible for primary schools in Basingstoke, I was tasked with responding to these findings. The respondents' views saddened me, reflecting experiences that school leaders would find disturbing. The more I learned about children's lived experiences, the more convinced I became of the need for long-term change. This was not a quick fix, and I had to explain the challenge to politicians and senior officers. Despite my discomfort and lack of experience in this area, I felt obligated to lead this work. It is an area I had never been involved with previously, and it made me feel quite uncomfortable. Who was I to challenge schools about how they respond to racist stereotypes and abuse? I was working outside my comfort zone and was concerned that I would offend those for whom I wanted to advocate.

Hearing and responding to the challenge

The context for our organisational development was on a large scale, as this district within a large local authority, encompassed 76 schools, of all phases and types, and involved the experiences of approximately 19 000 pupils. There was a political and social driver for change, responding to national and international movements. My strategy needed to respect those who shared their views and accept the challenges they faced. Balancing political and social expectations for positive change with the pressures on a school system still reeling from the pandemic was crucial.

As an adviser, when considering large-scale organisational change, it is important not to over-promise and under-deliver. Faced with politicians, councillors and vocal community groups, I felt under pressure to commit to driving change in all district schools – an easily promised but nearly impossible task through direct instruction. A quicker and more manageable approach would have been to find a specific area of improvement, such as to increase the number of schools recognising and recording racist incidents. This would provide straightforward data improvements to demonstrate a response to the challenge. However, I felt a broader approach was needed for large-scale organisational development.

Building the case for change

The challenge was to clearly define what needed development and how to deliver it effectively. I collaborated with colleagues to establish a comprehensive strategy that addressed the identified areas. I realised that I could attempt to 'fix' what I believed the issue to be without truly understanding causation and effect, so I needed to develop my own knowledge and understanding.

To bring about widespread organisational change, I recognised the importance of leveraging the strong professional relationships I had nurtured with headteachers. The local authority does not have the power to direct how schools operate in these areas; it relies on the power of influence. Despite advocating for significant change, headteachers were prepared to listen and saw that I was committed to investing my time and energy. They quickly agreed to get involved.

A critically important factor was the testimony of a black headteacher working in the district, which is uncommon in our southern shire county. Listening to his lived experiences as a child, during his route into teaching, and now in headship was humbling and reflected exactly what the inquiry had found.

I suggested and co-constructed the Basingstoke and Deane Inclusion and Diversity Partnership with headteachers, community representatives and the local authority. This partnership aimed for long-term goals, emphasising collaboration and growth and belonging. The precision of language was key, even down to our assertion that this should not be a project but a partnership, suggesting that we are working together, growing, but with no fixed endpoint.

The adviser as a facilitator for change

I recognised the need for an immediate response to energise stakeholders while committing to long-term change and managing real-time challenges. I drafted a local authority response focused on five areas:

- leadership;
- teaching and learning;
- voice;
- well-being and belonging;
- community.

The action plan outlined how the local authority would facilitate change and identified the commitments schools needed to make. The desired immediate impact was school engagement. At the launch event, 97% of district schools attended, where we shared the inquiry findings and the partnership's goals to work together on addressing them.

Data – friend or foe?

Surprisingly, there is no statutory requirement for schools in England to record prejudicial language or behaviour, though Ofsted expects it. Hampshire, aware of the risks in a more mono-cultural community, has a long history of collecting such data with schools' agreement. Actually, it is one of the few local authorities that collect this data from all schools, and this gives a strong basis to record the impact of the partnership annually. The voluntary annual reporting of this data, however, can place the local authority in a difficult position if higher numbers of incidents are reported. My experience in how data changes when there is a focus on an issue suggested that reporting could well increase as a response to raised awareness. High reporting shows challenge and recognition of the issue but can also generate 'click bait' headlines that could lead to reputational damage. Preparing stakeholders for what success might look like was crucial in the early stages.

We collated data on engagement levels, recorded incidents and schools signing the commitment document. As anticipated, the district saw a 174% increase in recorded racist incidents, the highest in the county, and a decline in schools reporting no incidents: down from 47% to 19% over the first 3 years of the partnership. This showed that schools were beginning to respond to the finding that schools dismissed incidents as insignificant. Analysis of academic outcomes also showed that over the first two years in the district, outcomes for black and minority ethnic students increased, against the trend for that group in the rest of the county. This points to the absolute need for transparency if we are to advocate for better equality for all our children, both in terms of academic outcomes and incidents of prejudicial language and behaviour.

The impact of the partnership

What has tangibly changed is the willingness of leaders within their own schools to embrace that uncomfortable feeling that I first felt. It takes courage to challenge social norms, recognising how others' lived experiences differ to our own; therefore, we need to think differently. The success of the partnership has spread across Hampshire, with 94 schools signing the commitment document and 89 Equality and Rights Advocates (EARA) pupil groups established in primary schools, up from just 7. The Inclusion and Diversity Partnership (IDP) website, hosted on the Hampshire County Council Improvement and Advisory Service's Moodle, contains a wealth of freely available resources linked to this work.

Evaluating my advisory impact on the schools' and district climate is challenging. I have grown more confident in discussing social and political issues and reporting at the county level. A county steering group and district groups are now in place, with headteachers embracing the challenge. More work is needed to tackle racial inequality and perhaps other issues, such as sexism and ableism. The relatively low level of recorded incidents may suggest similar underreporting.

Conclusion

In this chapter, I have taken a case study approach to reflect how education advisers can drive organisational development through:

- clarity of vision relating to political and social drivers for change;
- drawing on the knowledge and expertise of colleagues to set goals and strategy;
- influencing others through demonstrating commitment to the vision;
- using a variety of measures and planned performance indicators to reflect both short and long-term change.

Those who shared their experiences in the initial inquiry were surprised by the open-minded approach of education leaders when faced with challenging social and political views. Publicly accepting that we can and should do better has borne fruit in terms of building strong relationships with politicians, schools and wider stakeholder groups, driving positive change across the county – and the momentum is growing.

 Further reading

Akinde, F. (2024) *Be an Ally, Not a Bystander*. London: Corwin.

Boakye, J. (2022) *I Heard What You Said*. London: Picador.

Eddo-Lodge, R. (2018) *Why I Am No Longer Talking to White People about Race*. London: Bloomsbury Publishing.

Hampshire County Council Improvement and Advisory Service. *Inclusion and Diversity Partnership (IDP)*. Online at: https://hias-moodle.mylearningapp.com. (Accessed on 29/04/25).

Kara, B. (2021) *Diversity in Schools*. London: Sage.

Wilson, H., & Kara, B. (2022) *Diverse Educators: A Manifesto*. London: University of Buckingham Press.

6 Continuing to develop as an outstanding initial teacher training provider in the context of significant national change

LIZ BIRCHINALL

Key learning

- Keep your vision front and centre as you navigate the changes, especially when the changes are mandatory.
- Become fully informed and knowledgeable about all the requirements of the mandatory changes.
- Network with other educational providers as 'more heads are better than one'.
- Draw on robust programmes of self-evaluation underpinned with evidence from effective QA processes.
- Construct a realistic action plan with a timeline of deliverables and hard deadlines.
- Develop a strong staff team of independent self-starters so that you can delegate responsibilities, not just tasks.
- Pilot materials and processes and respond to feedback well in advance of deadlines for implementation.

AoEA criteria

- Criterion 22: Critically evaluates the design of the curriculum or educational offer
- Criterion 23: Is able to link vision, policy, strategy, plans, goals and ambitions to long-term requirements and immediate needs
- Criterion 24: Links the job design and people development to strategic requirements
- Criterion 25: Is able to analyse management procedures and systems
- Criterion 26: Is able to apply a variety of measurements of success and performance indicators

Introduction

The University of Manchester (UoM) primary postgraduate certificate of education (PGCE) is a one-year post-graduate teacher education programme leading to the award of the PGCE with qualified teacher status (QTS). On completion of the programme trainee teachers are recommended to the Department of Education (DfE) for the QTS while the academic element, the PGCE, is awarded by the University of Manchester. The UoM primary PGCE has an excellent reputation nationally and internationally and has been rated outstanding by Ofsted on three occasions, 2011, 2018 and 2024. The programme acts as a teacher supply chain into primary schools in the Northwest of England with approximately 80% of trainee teachers being employed within 20 miles of the university, and the remainder securing employment nationally and internationally.

Context

This case study outlines how the UoM primary PGCE leadership and management team responded to the significant changes in teacher education in England between 2019 to and 2024. These changes were mandated by the DfE for all providers of initial teacher training (ITT) in England. This chapter provides key learning and advice to address the organisational development and change process in a higher education context. A unique aspect of this case study is the complexity of managing with the multiple stakeholders involved in the primary PGCE programme, specifically:

the DfE

Ofsted

the UoM

the 150 primary partnership schools in Greater Manchester

Chronology of mandated changes

In 2019, the DfE published a statutory framework for initial teacher training called the Core Content Framework, 2019 (CCF). This is a statutory curriculum or 'syllabus' for all English accredited ITT providers. Following the report from the *Initial Teacher Training (ITT) market review: overview* (DfE, 2022) in England, all providers of ITT were required to undergo a two-year accreditation process should they wish to deliver ITT programmes from September 2024. Before implementation of the new framework, all accredited providers were also required to be inspected by Ofsted to ensure compliance. Figure 6.1 gives an overview and timeline of the statutory changes.

The UoM was one of only 80 providers who were successfully accredited through round 1, ready to deliver the new reformed ITT starting in September 2024. For the whole sector, this was a challenging time and required significant leadership and management skills to navigate the change management process.

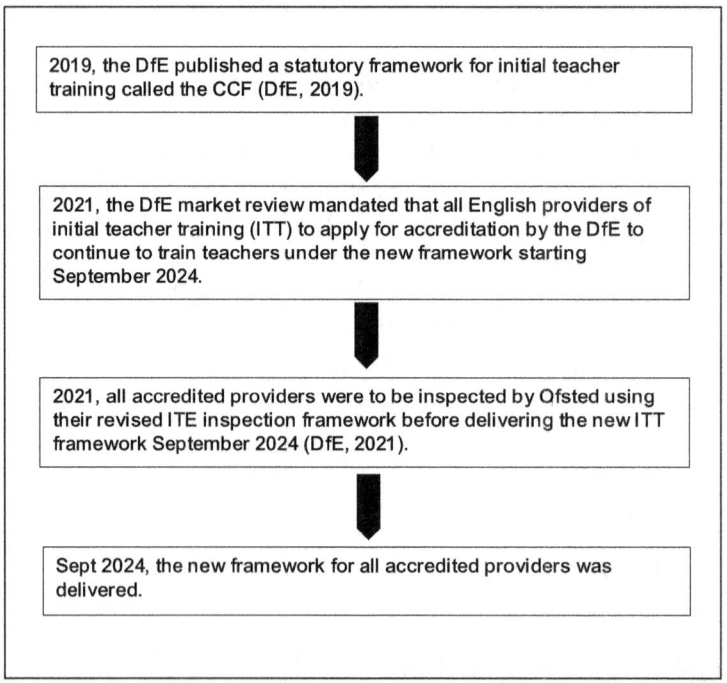

Figure 6.1 Timeline of statutory changes

Stages in the change management process

There are a range of change management models which generally follow a similar structure, for example (Fullan, 2016, p. 54), which was similar to our approach in this project, as exemplified in Figure 6.2.

Alongside the linear processes described, regular communication and consultation with multiple stakeholders resulted in non-linear developments as we responded to feedback from these parties. Change management is often not a linear process (Fullan, 2016), and this was definitely the case for us. Alongside the change management process, we were simultaneously preparing for the imminent Ofsted inspection.

Initiation stage for UoM primary PGCE

Values and vision

For programme leaders, it was important that we maintained fidelity with our programme vision. Our vision is to recruit the best applicants, train them to be the best teachers, so that pupils have the best education and thus life-changing opportunities. It was important that we consistently reflected on our values and principles as we

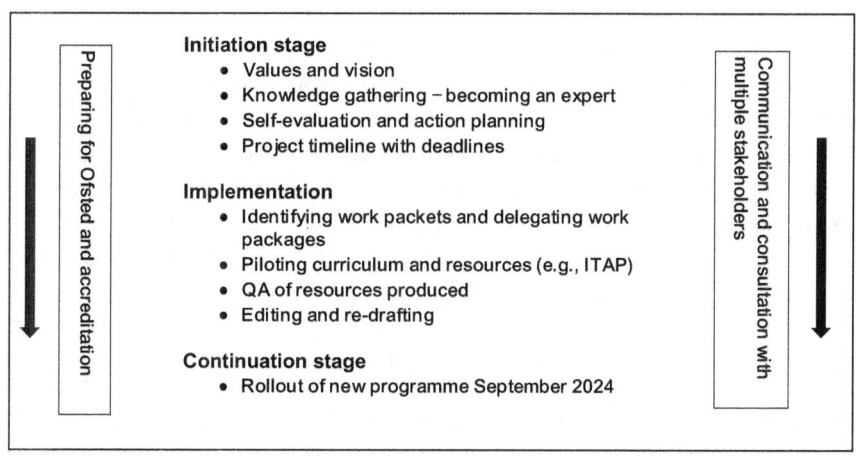

Figure 6.2 Fullan's change management model at work

implemented DfE directives ensuring that our decision-making processes adhered to our vision.

Become fully knowledgeable

It was crucial for the programme leadership team to become fully informed about all the DfE changes that were mandated. This involved reading many DfE documents, attending DfE training meetings and network meetings with providers. Becoming fully informed about the new requirements meant that our vision, strategies, plans and actions would lead to compliant implementation of the changes.

Communication

Staff and stakeholders needed to feel secure and well-led, particularly when the educational landscape around them was shifting considerably. Strong leadership with effective communication was key. This meant many meetings, discussions and emails to develop a clear shared message about the challenges faced internally and externally. It was also important that all stakeholders felt seen and heard in a collaborative process to ensure 'buy in' for the implementation and continuation stages of the process.

We talked to headteacher partners and set up working parties to share resources and asked for feedback. We consulted trainee teachers about the new curriculum (CCF) through student committee meetings and ongoing programme evaluations. We held frequent and regular staff meetings to draw on their expertise and experience in shaping the programme and meeting requirements. We met with senior leaders in the university to ensure that the core values of the university were still included in our new curriculum. We received regular feedback from the DfE about our progress.

Programme self-evaluation and action planning

The UoM Primary PGCE had pre-existing robust and rigorous self-evaluation procedures and action planning. This meant that we could draw on evidence to understand our outcomes, strengths and areas to improve and test these against the new statutory reforms.

We were able to identify gaps in our current curriculum, which did not incorporate CCF statutory statements, whilst retaining what was effective in our existing curriculum. We produced a realistic action plan with a timeline of deliverables and hard deadlines to track progress over time and adjust where necessary.

Implementation stage

Identifying work packets and delegating work packages

We are fortunate to have a dedicated, experienced and expert staff team. The staff team are independent self-starters, which means that you can delegate accountability for the work packages and not just tasks. This left the senior leadership team (SLT) free to maintain a strategic overview of the project knowing that the delegated work packages would be delivered by the required deadline.

Curriculum design

Our subject leaders are expert academics and primary school teachers who are knowledgeable and skilled in designing curricula. Consequently, they were able to amalgamate the new requirements of the CCF framework into our existing curriculum maintaining a high-quality and ambitious teacher training curriculum.

Piloting materials and seeking feedback well in advance of final deadlines

At all stages of the project, new materials produced were piloted with trainees, headteachers and mentors in schools and the DfE. This enabled us to receive feedback and edit drafts to ensure high quality and compliance with statutory requirements.

Continuation stage

In February 2024, we received confirmation that we had met all criteria for the accreditation of our programme. In May 2024, four months before the roll out of the new ITT framework, the University of Manchester Primary PGCE had its Ofsted inspection and was judged outstanding in all categories. With accreditation and a successful Ofsted, we were now able to roll out the new programme in September 2024.

Examples of challenges and solutions

On reflection, there were many moments of learning and development for us all in the case study described. In offering advice to others with similar challenges in similar contexts, there are two specific examples of challenge and demand that are worthy of consideration.

Challenge 1: Managing change with limited time resources

A recurring challenge was the demand on staff time and limited capacity. Staff were already busy with the normal 'day job' of running the programme, so the additional workload of preparing for an Ofsted inspection and completing the work for accreditation was challenging. The deadlines provided by the DfE for regular submissions were often short and frequently fell during traditional holiday periods.

How we managed this challenge:

- We prioritised work packages across all three elements: programme, DfE accreditation and Ofsted.
- We removed unnecessary work packages and rescheduled for later in the year or subsequent years.
- We divided work packages into smaller achievable tasks across as many staff as possible.
- We reassigned some tasks to build capacity where needed, for example, assignment marking.

Challenge 2: Unforeseen impact on existing systems

An unforeseen impact was the extensive editing required for all our existing programme documentation to incorporate the changes. This work package was immense and had far-reaching consequences for communication and training for all stakeholders, particularly the mentors who trained our trainees and the headteachers who hosted them.

How we addressed this:

- roadshow events with all Greater Manchester schools including headteachers and mentors;
- dedicated mentor training events to update them with the changes;
- frequent staff meetings to ensure alignment;
- regular meetings with the DfE to confirm compliance.

Conclusion

For other educational leaders in similar contexts with similar challenges, we recommend approaching the changes with alignment to your educational vision, robust self-evaluation, strategic prioritisation and a collaborative team-based approach.

There were three key factors which were critical to the success of this project. Firstly, our robust self-evaluation processes allowed us to identify strengths to maintain and areas that needed developing. Secondly, our staff's ability to take ownership of delegated responsibilities created the capacity needed to manage multiple demands made on us simultaneously. Thirdly, our commitment to involve all stakeholders through regular and clear communication ensured that changes were implemented with support from all involved.

If I were to pick one factor out of the many, the staff team is the most important. Recruiting staff, developing staff and providing staff with agency and opportunity has meant that they were able to address challenges when they were presented. Consequently, we had successful outcomes. Going forward as a programme, we can confidently live our vision of training the best teachers possible so pupils have the best life opportunities possible.

Chapter acknowledgements

I want to thank Dr Rebecca Phillips and senior lecturer Karen Kilkenny whose commitment, hard work, skill and expertise were key in achieving the success detailed in this chapter. These outcomes are as a direct result of their collective efforts and those of our wider PGCE team. I am very lucky to work alongside such great leaders and staff.

Further reading

DfE (2019) *Initial Teacher Training (ITT): Core Content Framework.* Online at: https://www.gov.uk/government/publications/initial-teacher-training-itt-core-content-framework. (Accessed on 04/02/25).

DfE (2021) *Initial Teacher Training (ITT) Market Review Report.* Online at: https://www.gov.uk/government/publications/initial-teacher-training-itt-market-review-report. (Accessed on 04/02/25).

DfE (2022) *Initial Teacher Training (ITT) Market Review: Overview.* DfE. Online at: https://www.gov.uk/government/publications/initial-teacher-training-itt-market-review/initial-teacher-training-itt-market-review-overview. (Accessed on 04/02/25).

References

Fullan, M. (2016) *The New Meaning of Educational Change.* New York Teachers College Press.

7 Developing the quality of SEND provision across a system of schools: A Northern Ireland case study

KIRSTY LOGAN-HALL

Key learning

- Inclusion improves outcomes for all learners.

- By embracing the opportunities to support all learners, we confidently develop the whole school community.

- A whole school system approach ensures children with SEND are taught in the right environment by the right people all of the time.

AoEA criteria

- Criterion 21: Understands the PESTLE drivers for change

- Criterion 23: Is able to link vision, mission, policy, strategy, resources, plans, goals and ambitions to long-term requirements and immediate needs

- Criterion 24: Is able to link job design and people development to strategic requirements

- Criterion 25: Is able to analyse management procedures and systems

Introduction

To develop the quality of Special Educational Needs and Disabilities (SEND) provision across a system of schools, we, first and foremost, must be aware of and transparent in relation to the changing landscape of children's needs and the impact that this is having on our day-to-day teaching and management in schools.

We, as school leaders and advisers working with leaders, need to embrace this situation from a strategic perspective and embark not only on a journey for our pupils but for our staff, for our whole school and wider community. We need to own this new norm of pupil population for our students.

We have an opportunity to connect the aspiration of inclusion and the vision of the Department of Education's strategy with how we work in partnership within our school, across our schools and with our wider education system.

This chapter sets out to examine how settings and the systems that support them can be developed to make education work for all.

Context

The aim of our current SEN Reform Agenda (2025) is to transform the provision for children with special educational needs in Northern Ireland. The comprehensive reform focuses on several key areas:

- *Greater inclusion*: ensuring children with SEN can participate in a mainstream education setting.
- *Early identification and intervention*: recognising and addressing educational needs promptly to provide timely support.
- *In-school and specialist support*: enhancing resources within schools and offering specialist services to cater to diverse pupil needs.
- *Workforce development*: investing in professional learning.

Its baseline reaffirms just how important a collective, shared response is, given that:

- One in five of our children and young people, 68,240 learners, are registered as having a special educational need and/or disability.
- Two decades have seen a 29% increase in children and young people with SEN and a 134% increase in those with a statement of SEN, that is 26,964 learners.

- Since 2017–18, the number of pupils with statements has risen by 38%, alongside an increase of 21% in pupils attending special schools.

Given this context, there is a keen ambition for pupils to be placed in a setting that meets both the needs of the child with SEN and the needs of their peers. One option for these children is to attend a special provision within a mainstream school, where small numbers of pupils of similar age and need learn together and integrate with their peer class regularly. Special provisions are housed within the school building, where possible, or within purpose-built modular accommodation, where necessary.

Modelling the vision in school

Within our own school, we believe we have created the right environment for all our children; we have a range of special provisions, and each child is able to learn and progress in a calm environment. Staff ensure intensive interaction activities daily to engage each child as he/she learns appropriate communication within a small-group special provision setting. The staff work together so that each child has the opportunity to integrate into the mainstream class where and when appropriate. When integrating into structured play, for example, the child is immersed into a language-rich environment where he/she learns from peers who model the appropriate interactions, rather than staff. We see first-hand the benefits for those communication skills. The children in the mainstream class build empathy and patience for others. We see these children form significant relationships with peers throughout the whole school.

Translating beliefs and values into action in school

We believe that all children should be able to attend their local primary school along with their siblings and neighbours. We believe that their local primary school should be and can be equipped to meet their needs. Just four years ago, when we began this development within our own school, our data showed the demand for suitable placement locally, and we knew a special provision within our school would better meet these needs and, therefore, better meet the needs of our whole school community. Creating a truly inclusive school begins with a shared staff belief that together, we make that inclusive school a reality.

In school, we identified a suitable space through a whole-school estate analysis. Patient and persistent negotiation brought about reconfiguration of the seldom-used employing authority offices on site. Very quickly, we had room to create that calm, supportive, breakout space for our SEN pupils. Subsequently, significant work was carried out to create the correct physical environment for our pupils.

When we talk about creating the correct environment, we know this goes beyond the structure. It's about the context and the climate for learning in its entirety: staffing, including support staff internal and external; pupils; and the systems and structures underpinning the learning across the whole school community. Tullygally Primary School is a nurturing school. Most of the staff have been trained in trauma-informed practice, skills that are easily transferred when working with SEN pupils. From the outset, the decision was made to staff the special provision with existing staff with the desire for this additional provision to feel part of the school and not a separate unit. We wanted the children to integrate; we wanted the staff to integrate. We wanted the staff to strengthen its capacity for an effective inclusive education throughout the whole school.

Within the special provision staff receive professional learning from a range of services; other staff within the school join these sessions building their capacity, which, in turn, is developing a wider, competent and confident staff. All teachers and support staff are equipped with knowledge and skills to work effectively with pupils with SEN, wherever they are deployed. This builds a culture of learning together, supporting each other and having those conversations which enable each child to access the best form of support promptly. Staff can see their own development and the role they play in creating the right environment for these pupils, and they can see how well that works. Staff within the school get support from staff within the special provision when they or their pupils need it. Informed support is given in a timely manner with early intervention, on site.

We have now been on this journey for four years and are rapidly increasing and developing. As a school leadership team, we make decisions about the works being carried out so that all our pupils will benefit. At a time when budgets are tight, this is a way to ensure resources can be organised to support all the school's pupils. We now have a wonderful facility which has raised the school profile and is celebrated in and beyond our community.

Vision into action across the system

Having succeeded in realising the strategy's aims in our own setting, much of my current role is now in advising and supporting policy-makers, services and school leaders in understanding and defining vision as tangible action. Because we have led this transition successfully in school, we are able to articulate clearly why and how we began a process where we moved from passion to practice. In the midst of all that needs to be developed within the SEND arena, I can prioritise and advise on the development of one targeted key area of focus with system colleagues. Then, together, we can prioritise and progress another. Examples include enhanced professional learning for SEN staff, how to expedite access to external services and developing an equitable classroom assistant model.

Similarly, this work involves explaining and modelling some SEN structures and systems that work well, identifying areas that do not work and the accumulative benefits of responsive development and effective deployment of staff. We can showcase and explain the development of our staff to peer colleagues and develop their understanding of the benefits for pupils and families across a system of schools. We can explain that in making the most of the professional learning for a handful of staff, we can build the capacity of all our staff. This builds resilience and sustainability within our settings. We have a finite resource. I advise on how we can flex that resource, making it work better for the child. When it works better for the child, it seems to work better for the staff and for the school. And when it works for every child and every school, it works better for us all.

While most, if not all, schools have pupils who benefit from some additional breakout space, many schools do not have ready-made space or indeed any unused space at all. It is important to understand these contextual challenges and to support these settings in finding a solution that works for them. Many benefit from our experience by simply getting to see how we have tailored the space we have and hearing how we develop and integrate our staff and pupils. Professional conversations with school leaders and services in themselves unravel new possibilities. For policy-makers, professional discussions deepen awareness of system flexibility, that some school estates can be reconfigured while others need greater investment.

The voice of the child has been enshrined in policy and law for many years. That voice, though, is often unheard. As school leaders and as system leaders, we each have a voice. Our work builds and strengthens the systems of communication between schools and services, between schools and policy-makers and between schools themselves. As experienced school leaders, we are the builders of the system. Our many years of practice, experience and observations of when and how the system is working or is not working for our children and young people means we are well-placed to amplify strongly the voices of our children and young people when they need us to. We believe that we have a responsibility and an opportunity to use our voice and build the systems emanating from policy that make education work for all our pupils and, equally, for all our staff.

Conclusion

Having a special provision within your school brings significant benefits for professional development and growth. Staff build both their capacity and strong networks for professional collaboration across schools and services. Staff learn first-hand how to support these children fully and adapt approaches to the benefit of all learners. They create a professional learning community to share resources and strategies, ensuring that all pupils, regardless of their needs, have access to high-quality teaching and learning. In Tullygally, we ensure our children are placed correctly so that their needs are met and that all our children begin their learning journey in an environment where they feel safe, secure and happy.

We have the aspiration to strengthen and to develop further the quality of SEN provision across our whole school system; we want all our children and young people to be able to learn and grow. Similarly, we want to work in an education system where we feel valued, supported and developed properly for the job in hand; we want all our staff to learn and grow. We want to be able to confidently support all our children and young people so they develop to their optimum and are given that opportunity to succeed and thrive. In education, learning on the job is okay. In fact, it's more than okay, it can be transformational.

References

Department of Education NI (2025) *Truly Equal, Valuably Different: Special Educational Needs Reform Agenda.* Bangor: Department of Education.

Further reading

Bomber, L. M., & Hughes, D. A. (2013) *Settling to Learn.* Broadway: Worth Publishing.

Boxall, M. (2010) *Nurture Groups in Schools: Principle and Practice.* London: Sage Publications Ltd.

Gill, N., & Darley, H. (2018) *Creating Change in Urban Settings.* Norwich: Singular Publishing.

Kotter, J. P. (2012) *Leading Change.* Brighton: Harvard Business Review Press.

Maslow, A. H. (2018) *A Theory of Human Motivation.* VA: Wilder Publications.

Part 2
Planning for organisational effectiveness

8 The importance of the strategic plan in aligning planning, people and performance

PETER PARISH

Key learning

- The organisational development model provides a framework for supporting an organisation with the alignment of its strategy, people and processes in a systematic way.

- Strategic planning and improvement planning should always be sharply focused on delivering to the needs of the organisation.

- Leadership has a key role in establishing the values within an organisation and in facilitating alignment.

- All strategic developments should take into account the capacity of the staff of the organisation to successfully deliver change.

AoEA criteria

- Criterion 21: Understands the PESTLE drivers for change

- Criterion 22: Critically evaluates the design of the curriculum or educational offer

- Criterion 23: Is able to link vision, policy, strategy, plans, goals and ambitions to long-term requirements and immediate needs

- Criterion 24: Links the job design and people development to strategic requirements

- Criterion 25: Is able to analyse management procedures and systems

- Criterion 26: Is able to apply a variety of measurements of success and performance indicators

- Criterion 27: Is able to assess the context for organisational improvement

Introduction

In this chapter, I will look at how strategic planning is enhanced by being underpinned by a holistic model of organisational development which aligns planning, people and performance. The approach will be illustrated with some practical examples.

Schools and other organisations are often bombarded with new initiatives and developments. The challenge for leaders and those giving advice is to make sense of the organisation's development needs in a coherent way. Planning and interventions can often focus on one area of activity, and leaders can miss considering the impact on the organisation as a whole.

The Chartered Institute of Personnel Development (CIPD) has used the following definition for organisational development:

> *a planned and systematic approach to enabling sustained organisational performance through the involvement of its people.*
>
> (CIPD, 2025)

Within the AoEA, we have used this definition to inform the design of the organisational development framework illustrated in Figure 8.1.

The organisational development model provides a framework for supporting an organisation to be fit for both today's world and tomorrow's through the alignment of its strategy, people and processes in a systematic way. It enables the link between vision, policy, strategy, plans, goals and ambitions to long-term requirements and immediate needs.

The model of organisational development reminds us of the six external factors that impact on all the workings of the organisation. As discussed in an earlier chapter, these are often referred to as PESTLE – the political, economic, social, technological, legal and environmental factors, which are forever changing. Organisational development advisers can have a key role to play in enabling school leaders to be mindful of the changing external factors affecting its organisation and how this influences strategic thinking.

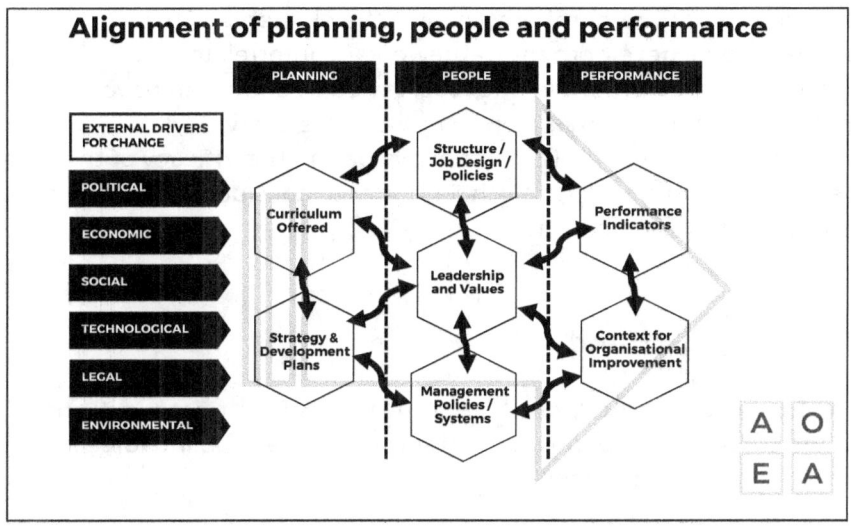

Figure 8.1 Aligning planning, people and performance

How the organisational development framework assists in the alignment of planning, people and performance

The organisational development framework takes three overarching strands: PLANNING – PEOPLE – PERFORMANCE.

Each strand comprises a number of elements:

- 'Planning' covers the curriculum offered, strategy and development plans.
- The 'people' strand covers leadership and values; structure, job design and policies; management policies and systems.
- 'Performance' covers performance indicators and the context for organisational improvement.

The organisational development framework also helps with understanding and analysing complexity. Unpicking each strand helps to ensure consistency and coherence across the whole framework. In essence, strategic planning needs to take into account both external (PESTLE) and internal (PLANNING – PEOPLE – PERFORMANCE) influences on an organisation's development.

It is important to remember that all of the elements of the organisational development framework are interrelated. So, a change or development in one area, say curriculum, can have implications for the other elements. With this overview, the adviser can play a key role in either evaluating the efficacy of the development or coaching a school leader to consider the full impact of a strategic development.

The 'people' strand

'Leadership and values', which lie at the heart of the framework and at the centre of the 'people' strand should be the enabling force in the implementation of strategy.

The 'Strategy Pyramid' (McGuinness, 2012) in Figure 8.2 nicely summarises the strategic planning process.

Strategic planning and improvement planning should always be sharply focused on delivering to the needs of the organisation. The first three tiers are crucial in driving the last three, and it is always worthwhile spending time to get these clear as they are crucial in underpinning decisions. Needless to say, establishing these must

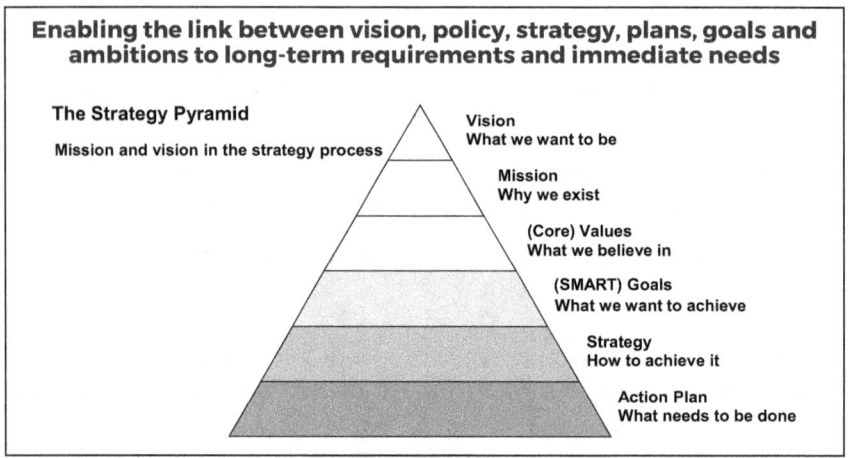

Figure 8.2 The Strategy Pyramid

involve key stakeholders in the organisation. Advisers can help leaders to enable the link between vision, policy, strategy, plans, goals and ambitions. In doing so, they can help to ensure plans address both long-term requirements and immediate needs.

Structure, job design and policies

People development is critical within organisations. Organisations need to develop their people to meet the needs of the strategy. This has implications for training, professional learning and staffing. Staff must have the experience, skills and ability to do what the leadership is now asking them to do. The leadership needs to ensure that the staffing structure is fit for the present, the organisation's next steps, and not the past. Leaders need to be sure when embarking on a new initiative that staff have the necessary knowledge and skills to succeed.

Management policies and systems

The systems within an organisation are a major link between its strategic vision and its required outcomes. Systems and processes should facilitate getting the right job done with minimal bureaucracy. Management, therefore, requires effective systems and procedures. Organisations need to be clear about the 'command and supply chain'. For example, to consider the part Information and Communication Technology will play within the strategy and to what extent it is integral.

It is also important to risk-assess the major system issues that could be faced in delivering change to the curriculum and support services. Any particular financial issues related to this situation need to be identified. How will income and expenditure be affected? Clarity is also needed regarding legal and commercial partnership agreements and protocols to ensure they are good enough to operate within the transition. A risk assessment of the financial implications needs to be completed. New savings and new sources of expenditure should be identified.

> **Areas for the adviser to explore**
>
> How has the leadership ensured there is capacity within the workforce to improve performance? Is professional learning helping to ensure staff are being kept up-to-date and trained with the skills and knowledge needed to ensure success for all its students? To what extent are management policies and practices enabling the staff to be effective in operational delivery?

The planning strand

The design of the curriculum or service offer

For schools, this strand would predominantly relate to the curriculum. For support organisations, it would mainly be about the service offered. The curriculum sits at the heart of the educational offer. In most jurisdictions, it receives a major inspection focus in determining the quality of education within a school. The adviser can help to evaluate the design and the effectiveness of the curriculum. The curriculum, with its staffing requirements, also puts pressure on budgets. For instance, the decision to introduce a new subject will have longer-term staffing and, therefore, financial implications. The AoEA has developed a range of tools for the application of curriculum-led financial planning (CLFP). Efficiencies secured through CLFP will also help to provide resources to more effectively meet school improvement needs. It all helps to ensure that students are learning the right things and within budget.

Leaders need to decide how much resource they are going to devote to developing a new offer. The curriculum does not stay static, and leaders need to respond to shifting expectations. Advisers can help leaders realign resources to bring new delivery mechanisms into play. PESTLE, SWOT and risk analyses can be used to underpin the basis for both strategic planning (long-term requirements) and action planning (immediate needs). The AoEA has developed an interactive tool to support the management of risk within organisations.

> **Areas for the adviser to explore**
>
> Planning priorities – why has the leadership taken the decisions it has to shape the curriculum that students are offered? How is this reflected in the strategy and development plans that are driving activities across the organisation and its interaction with partners?

The 'performance' strand – performance and success indicators

Any strategic development will need to be underpinned by the application of a variety of measurements of success and performance indicators. Identifying which are the most significant for the well-being and future development of the organisation is essential. Many plans in organisations lack clarity in relation to their success criteria and key performance indicators, and the adviser can scrutinise plans to support and challenge this. A useful piece of advice – plan backwards from the destination before identifying the strategy that will deliver the long- and short-term objectives.

While crucially important, the measure of an organisation's success isn't just about 'scores on the doors', important though they are. Crucially, a school is also about many other things, such as:

- the development of responsible citizenship;
- students' ability to exercise good moral values and judgement.

Context for organisational development

'Softer' data analysis, such as questionnaires and interviews to gauge student, parental and community voice, help to explore some of these issues in relation to how it feels to live and work in the organisation and to explore the moral compass of its leaders more fully. Within the AoEA, we use a Context for Organisational Improvement survey to identify factors which might negatively affect staff motivation.

> **Areas for the adviser to explore**
>
> How is the leadership intent on judging the effectiveness of its strategic and operational decisions? How are staff responding to strategic and operational decisions? How are staff involved in helping to inform future strategy?

Applying the organisational development framework

The model can be used to support strategic alignment in contexts from local authority service planning to whole school planning, and to individual curriculum area planning.

Example 1: Local authority education service realignment

To cite one example, a local authority education service was supported to review and revise its offer in the light of the changing external context including the increased devolution of finance and accountability to schools and away from central provision. In a planning workshop, staff from different service areas were asked to consider the model and the implications for their area. This had a major impact on helping the staff teams to understand the necessity for change and contribute to planning. As a result, the staffing was re-aligned with future planning and change was successfully enacted more easily.

What follows, in Table 8.1, is an outline of the type of questions or prompts that were used to support and challenge thinking for this strategic change.

Table 8.1 Questions to support LA review of its service offer

Context	• In understanding the context, what are the key drivers for change?
	• Whatever model is developed must be based on firm foundations – why are we doing this in the first place?
	• Is this driven by government policy or a wider collaborative vision?
	• Have leaders, governors and key change agents really been engaged in understanding these key strategic needs?
Service/Curriculum Offer	• To what extent is the new development 'added on' to present structures or will the associated organisation infrastructure delivering this be reviewed?
	• Is the curriculum or service offer the right one? What services are being provided now? How do they need to be developed or even replaced?
	• Is the curriculum/service offer fit for purpose?
	• What opportunities are there to ensure that the curriculum/service is more responsive to need?
	• What are the risks that need to be managed?
Strategy and Plans	• Where is this development within the planning framework of the organisation, individual learning providers and schools?
	• Is what is being developed going to be around for a long time?
	• How will plans assist sustainable improvement in every child's interests?
Structure and Job Design	• Has the time been taken to define what staff skills and knowledge are required?
	• How will any skill deficit be addressed?
	• How will an appropriate structure be addressed with roles and responsibilities focused on the right things?

Leadership and Values	• Are the organisation's values explicit and shared? • Are there ways in which they need to be re-visited or re-ignited in the context of this change? • Do senior leaders have the competencies and leadership skills to respond to the direction of travel or a 'new' development? • Have leaders considered the dominant style of leadership they are going to apply when responding to this 'new' initiative? Directive, visionary, affiliative, democratic, modelling, coaching?
Management Policies and Systems	• Will the systems and processes to be put in place ensure an efficient delivery of the key objectives? • Are they enabling or do they inhibit efficiency? • Are they affordable in the long- and short-term?
Performance Indicators	• Have the most significant 'hard' and 'soft' performance indicators been identified? • Will any new model have a limited number of key performance indicators to assist in optimising focus?
Context for Organisational Improvement (COI)	• Is there a mechanism in place for checking on the effect leaders are having on improving the COI and how much they are improving that year on year so that 'what it is like to work here' is having even more impact in a year's time than it is now?

Example 2: Setting up a new educational provision

Another example of how the model helped to inform strategic planning was in the development of a different type of a school; a University Technology College, as it was termed. One key contextual driver was government policy to introduce new provision focused on high-quality science and engineering education to attract more young people into careers in these areas.

This specialist provision was sponsored by a university and attracted government grant funding to set it up. A project planning group was set up involving senior university staff and engineering industry experts and supported by an education consultancy/advisory team.

The strands of the OD model, its 'planning', 'people' and 'performance' all needed to be aligned to successfully open the provision. Central to the plan was the appointment of a principal. The planning group had defined the values and mission in the application, and these were then added to by the principal once appointed (**People** – Leadership and Values).

The next stage was to design a curriculum which would meet the aims of the college and, at the same time, be financially viable (**Planning** – Curriculum Offered). The staffing structure was then determined using a curriculum financial planning model, in which student numbers and therefore staffing grow in a phased way year-on-year. Once agreed, the practical process of constructing job descriptions and recruitment was undertaken. This, in turn, was followed by staff development to create a cohesive team with an understanding of and commitment to the core values of the college (**People** – Structure and Job Design).

As a new development, a whole range of policies, procedures and systems needed to be put in place (**People** – Management Policies and Systems). Systems for student progress monitoring were established to begin to prepare for external examinations (**Performance** – Indicators).

Once the college opened and started to operate, feedback systems were established to get the views of staff and to modify systems where necessary (**Performance** – COI).

The entire project was guided by a substantial development plan supported by a risk register (**Planning** – Strategy and Development Plans).

Example 3: Application of the framework to smaller-scale initiatives

The framework is applicable to informing smaller- or larger-scale initiatives. For instance, a primary school might want to introduce a new reading scheme perhaps in response to a political policy priority. Clearly, this has curriculum implications. The scheme would need to be costed and an implementation plan put in place. The leadership would have made the decision to change the reading scheme and introduced this to staff and governors. There would be a need for staff professional learning to ensure all staff had the necessary understanding and skills to deliver the new scheme. Systems would need to be put in place for the organisation of resources and assessment and tracking systems to identify and support pupils not reaching their potential. There would need to be some performance indicators identified for progress monitoring and accountability. It would also make sense for the leadership to get feedback from staff about their feelings about the scheme and what difference it was making.

Conclusion

When introducing or advising on a new initiative or development, the use of the organisational development model can help to provide coherence across planning, people and performance. Many of my colleagues at the AoEA and I have used the model for many years. Because the framework starts with consideration of the current and likely future PESTLE context, it always remains relevant. When dealing with any initiative or change, maximum impact will be achieved when the elements of the three strands – planning, people and performance – are aligned. This implies maximising the impact of resources and expertise for the benefit of learners. The framework also helps to identify areas of non-alignment and weaknesses and thereby key risks that must be mitigated to achieve the intended outcomes. At a basic level, the model provides an aide-mémoire when reviewing an initiative or development to ensure all bases are covered. It provides a framework to guide planning and for the adviser to ask relevant questions such as, 'Do staff have the relevant skills and expertise to make this initiative a success, and will it help us to improve outcomes?'

 References

Chartered Institute of Personnel and Development (CIPD) Website (2025) *What Is Organisation Development?* Online at: https://www.cipd.org/uk/knowledge/factsheets/organisational-development-factsheet. (Accessed on 01/04/25).

McGuinness, W. (2012) *The Origins of the Strategy Pyramid*. Online at: The Origins of the Strategy Pyramid – McGuinness Institute. (Accessed on 06/05/25).

9 Developing an effective, compassionate and inclusive curriculum

NARINDER GILL

Key learning

- Curriculum design should place compassion and inclusivity at the heart of learning.

- Understanding people, places, and environment is important in shaping curriculum decisions.

- A context-responsive curriculum promotes equity and social justice.

- Adopt practical strategies for co-creating curriculum frameworks with stakeholders.

- As an adviser, seek to influence curriculum reform across multiple schools and sustain change when not physically present.

- Adopt strategies for managing resistance, engaging hearts and minds and ensuring long-term impact.

AoEA criteria

- Criterion 22: Critically evaluates the design of the curriculum or educational offer

- Criterion 23: Is able to link vision, mission, policy, strategy, resources, plans, goals and ambitions to long-term requirements and immediate needs

- Criterion 24: Links job design and people development to strategic requirements

- Criterion 27: Is able to assess the context for organisational improvement

Introduction: compassion, purpose, and systemic impact

What does it mean to create a curriculum that is not only effective but truly compassionate and inclusive?

At a time when the purpose of education is under renewed scrutiny, this chapter proposes that curriculum is a moral and cultural act. It reflects who we are, what we value, and what we hope our children will become. Brighouse and Woods (2013) emphasise that a school's culture should uphold each child's dignity and foster ambitious aspirations for their future.

At Elevate Multi-Academy Trust, we have embraced that ambition.

We set out not simply to design a 'curriculum' but to shape a culture of belonging, of hope, and of wisdom.

Our work began with children: their stories, their communities, and it was built into a structured, evidence-informed framework that could be adapted across many schools whilst holding fast to core values.

This chapter is designed to support educational advisers who are working across multiple schools to build compassionate, inclusive cultures through curriculum. It offers a practical and reflective guide to leading change through influence, not control, where the role of the adviser is not to impose answers but to create the conditions in which the right questions are asked. Drawing on lived experience and grounded in the principles of system leadership, it shows how advisers can build trust, align vision with values, and embed sustainable frameworks that hold firm while remaining responsive to local context.

The shift from one school to many: leading with influence, not control

In headship, I was immersed in the day-to-day culture. My influence was immediate, visible. But system leadership demanded a different approach: less about doing and directing, more about enabling.

This is where educational advisers must develop a new toolkit:

- *Facilitation over direction*. My role shifted from curriculum 'driver' to one who creates the climate and scaffolding for others to lead.
- *Influence through narrative*. I relied more on storytelling, connecting curriculum intent to personal and professional purpose.
- *Knowing when to step back*. System leadership involves trusting others to lead within a shared framework. That required me to relinquish control while ensuring clarity of vision.

Key advisory lesson: system change happens through people, not papers. You cannot simply cascade a model and expect ownership. Instead, you must build a compelling moral case, provide structure, and then, step back, creating conditions for others to lead.

Understanding context: people, place, and environment

Dylan Wiliam (2018) reminds us that *'everything works somewhere, but nothing works everywhere'* (p. 45). This highlights that no single curriculum model can be universally effective. Context shapes every decision, making it critical to designing a curriculum that is responsive to the specific realities of the school community (Waters, 2019). This case study explores how Elevate Multi-Academy Trust developed a curriculum framework that balances consistency with flexibility, ensuring all children receive a high-quality education shaped by their unique community.

Elevate Multi-Academy Trust serves a diverse range of schools across North Yorkshire, each with distinct contextual factors:

- *Rural village schools*: small pupil populations, strong community ties, and limited exposure to cultural diversity.
- *Market-town primary schools*: a mix of long-standing agricultural traditions and a growing commuter population.
- *Urban schools*: high proportions of pupils with socio-economic challenges.

Despite operating under one trust, each school required tailored curriculum adaptations to ensure learning was meaningful, relevant, and aspirational.

Our curriculum design principles

We committed to a model that balanced a framework with flexibility. This was not a centralised prescription but a shared spine. It gave schools a clear progression model and language but allowed local adaptation.

Our principles:

- deeply contextual;
- co-constructed with all stakeholders;
- coherent across phases and subjects;
- committed to social justice and high expectations for all.

This encouraged schools to see the curriculum model not as something done to them but something done with them and for their children. Figure 9.1 provides an illustration of the framework that we adopted.

Curriculum as co-creation

A defining feature of our work was the move from curriculum delivery to curriculum co-creation. We engaged multiple stakeholders in the design process:

- Children's voice was central, shaping topic choices, informing adaptations, and identifying gaps.
- Parents and community played a key role through community curriculum conversations and feedback loops.
- Subject leaders of education appointed across the Trust acted as curriculum architects, facilitating cross-school collaboration, ensuring coherence, and building capacity.

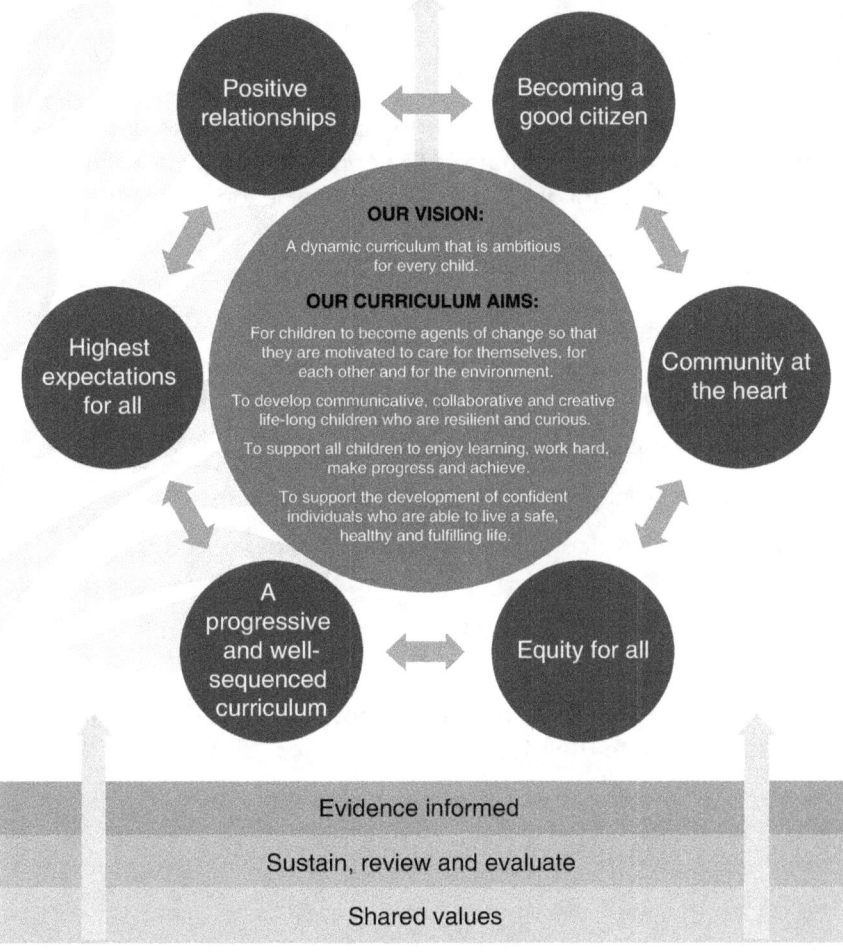

Figure 9.1 Curriculum framework (Gill, 2022, p. 3)

This collaborative design approach helped dismantle the binary between centralisation and autonomy, replacing it with a model of 'anchored flexibility'.

Using a focused framework to guide but not constrain thinking

Advisers can use this as a cultural entry point – before speaking about curriculum, listen for what matters to people in that place. Brighouse and Woods (1999) highlight the significance of leaders who engage in thoughtful questioning to promote reflective practice among educators (Brighouse & Woods, 1999, p. 160).

We began with curiosity, not assumption.

Key questions that guided our approach:

- What do we mean by curriculum?
- What do we teach and why?
- How does our curriculum reflect the lived experiences of our children and families?
- What is special about our community, and how does this link to our school values?
- How do we empower children with knowledge, skills, and cultural capital relevant to their futures?
- How do we incorporate community voices into curriculum design?

We built our framework, as illustrated in Figure 9.2, through the three lenses of:

- *People*. Who are our children, staff, and families? What stories do they bring?
- *Place*. What does the local community offer? What's its heritage, tension, and potential?
- *Environment*. What barriers or enablers affect educational opportunity?

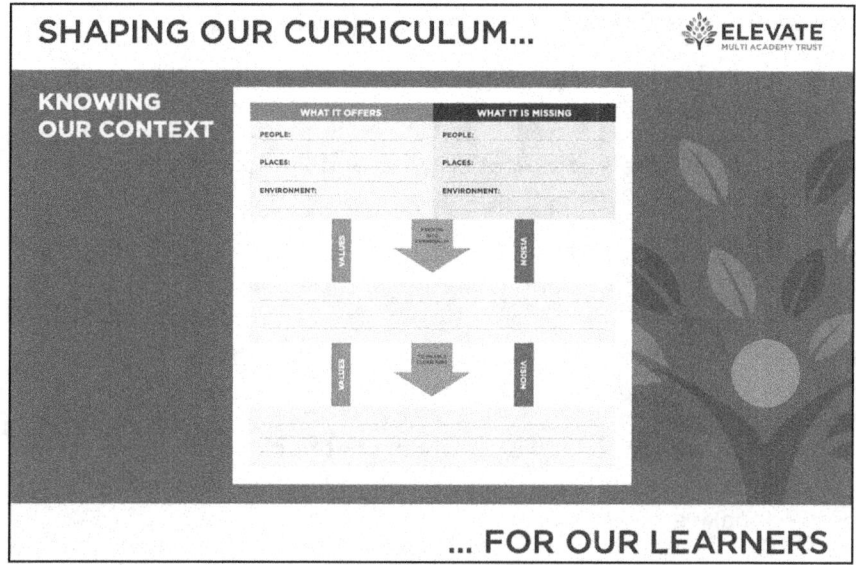

Figure 9.2 Shaping our curriculum (Gill, 2022, p. 1)

Phases of implementation

Phase 1: Deep contextual understanding (2019–2022)

This phase helped dismantle deficit thinking and reframed each community as rich in potential. It grounded the curriculum in lived reality, acknowledging what children bring, not just what they lack.

- Curriculum design templates required mapping of local knowledge, strengths, and gaps.
- They challenged deficit thinking and reframed communities as curriculum assets.
- They used data and stories to inform curriculum decisions: a blend of evidence and emotion.
- They linked school-level insights to broader trust-wide curriculum ambitions.

Phase 2: Progression and coherence (2022–2023)

Subject progression documents were co-written with leaders from across the trust:

- Curriculum leaders of education were appointed to act as subject specialists and peer coaches.
- Vocabulary progression was introduced as a trust-wide equity lever, based on research around word gap and life chances.

Phase 3: Pedagogy and continuous improvement (2023 to the present)

This final phase embedded a culture of continuous curriculum improvement, supported by subject networks and sustained professional learning, it:

- ensured curriculum implementation aligned with trust-wide teaching, learning and assessment (TLA) principles;
- embedded subject networks for ongoing reflection, development, and professional learning;
- used evidence (including book scrutiny, learning walks, and pupil voice) to refine and evolve the curriculum offer.

Advisory strategies: sustaining change when you're not in the room

Presence isn't always physical; it's cultural. To sustain curriculum reform across many schools, advisers need a deliberate strategy. Here's what worked:

- *Distributed Leadership*. By empowering curriculum leaders and subject networks, we created a web of influence that extended far beyond my own reach. These leaders became the heartbeat of change: modelling, coaching, and championing from within. They drove the momentum and adapted the model within their own schools.
- *Cultural leadership*. Using storytelling, real examples from schools and children to illustrate why change was needed. Data convinces

minds, but stories move hearts. This helped build intrinsic motivation.
- *Structured yet flexible implementation*. We offered clear progression frameworks and training but avoided rigid prescription. Schools were trusted to contextualise, balancing fidelity with autonomy.
- *Visible learning loops*. Regular meetings, virtual drop-ins, peer reviews, celebration events all built in visibility and momentum.
- *Psychological safety*. We ensured no one felt exposed. Innovation was encouraged, and learning from mistakes was normalised.

Navigating resistance and building momentum

Every transformation invites challenge. We anticipated and responded to barriers with compassion and clarity:

- *Lean into resistance with curiosity*. Rather than dismiss pushback, I engaged in coaching-style conversations to understand the root of concern. Was it fear of capability? Loss of autonomy? Misalignment with values?
- *Build early wins*. Small, visible successes such as the impact of vocabulary progression on pupil outcomes helped to shift narratives from scepticism to belief.
- *Communicate with integrity*. I was open about what we didn't know and transparent about why we were making certain decisions. Honesty built trust.
- *Use the power of proximity*. Even when I couldn't be in every school, I stayed connected through coaching sessions, listening events, and milestone celebrations.

Impact and reflections

We have seen measurable impact:
- All schools now have a curriculum shaped by community context.

- There is now greater alignment between curriculum, pedagogy, and assessment.
- Subject networks are thriving, led by staff across the trust.
- Children are more articulate, confident, and connected to their learning.
- Staff report increased confidence and clarity.

But more importantly, we've seen a shift in culture: from curriculum as coverage to curriculum as connection.

What I learnt not to do:

- Don't push ahead when people aren't ready. Urgency without readiness leads to burnout, not sustainable change.
- Don't confuse silence with buy-in. True engagement requires dialogue, not just compliance.
- Don't assume that everyone sees the moral imperative. Sometimes we have to make it visible through story and example.

Conclusion: curriculum as a compassionate act

As advisers and leaders, we are not just implementing strategy; we are shaping the culture of schools and the life chances of children.

A truly compassionate curriculum is one that:

- says to every child: 'You belong';
- enables every teacher to lead with clarity and purpose;
- builds community, hope, and resilience in a fragile world.

For any adviser working across schools: begin with people, stay curious, be clear about values, and always lead with heart.

Further reading

Brighouse, T. (2007) *How Successful Headteachers Survive and Thrive*. RM Publications (UK).

Waters, M. (2019) *Thinking Allowed: On School Leadership*. London: John Catt Educational.

West, M. (2021) *Compassionate Leadership: Sustaining Wisdom, Humanity and Presence in Health and Social Care*. London: Swirling Leaf Press.

 References

Brighouse, T., & Woods, D. (2013) *The A-Z of School Improvement*. London: Bloomsbury.

Brighouse, T., & Woods, D. (1999) *How to Improve Your School*. London: Routledge.

Gill, N. (2022) Of Elevate Multi-Academy Trust: Internal documents by Narinder Gill (the then Director of School Improvement).

- 2022 – Curriculum Framework (Figure 9.1).

- 2022 – Shaping Our Curriculum (Figure 9.2).

Wiliam, D. (2018) *Creating the Schools Our Children Need: Why What We're Doing Now Won't Help Much (and What We Can Do Instead)*. West Palm Beach, FL: Learning Sciences International.

10 Advising on the management of effective and sustainable curriculum design

KEVIN MCDERMID

Key learning

- Organisational Development Advisers have a key role to play in supporting an evaluation of the content of a school's curriculum plan in relation to the vision and principles of its curriculum intent.

- They are also well placed to support leaders in having a greater understanding of, and ability to apply, key elements of integrated curriculum and financial planning (ICFP).

AoEA criteria

Criterion 22: Can critically evaluate the design of the curriculum or educational offer

Criterion 23: Is able to link vision, policy, strategy, plans, goals and ambitions to long-term requirements and immediate needs

Criterion 25: Is able to analyse management procedures and systems

Introduction

The last two or three years have seen a major focus on curriculum reform in all four countries of the United Kingdom. Major strategic curriculum reviews at government level are taking place currently in Scotland, Wales, Northern Ireland and England. As a result, many educational leaders at every level are heavily involved in reviewing and, in many cases, radically modifying the principles, design and implementation of the curriculum in their own schools. Inevitably, some have found the management of curriculum change challenging, so the role of the adviser is crucial in providing support for the process at all levels.

DOI: 10.4324/9781003655176-15

At the same time, while there have been some advances over the last few years in addressing budget management in schools, including, in England, the deployment of nationally appointed school resource management advisers, schools and groups of schools still face significant challenges in ensuring their curriculum offer is affordable against a background of diminishing resource.

The role of the adviser, therefore, in evaluating the design of the curriculum, is to support a school, or a group of schools, in planning an effective, sustainable, high-quality curriculum offer within the constraints of available finance. The aim of this chapter is to suggest an approach and a range of questions that might help an adviser support schools through the process.

Curriculum intent

Curriculum intent refers to the overarching vision and principles that shape and guide the design and implementation of a school's curriculum.

A well-defined curriculum intent should encompass several key elements:

- *Vision*: the aspirations and expectations that the school has for its students, including the desired outcomes of their education.
- *Principles*: the fundamental beliefs and values that underpin the curriculum, guiding the teaching and learning processes.
- *Goals*: specific targets that the curriculum aims to achieve, such as academic excellence, personal development and social responsibility.
- *Strategy*: the approach and methods adopted to deliver the curriculum, ensuring it is both effective and sustainable.

For example, in Education Wales' *Curriculum for Wales 2025*, under the heading 'Curriculum design and the four purposes', the aim of a school's curriculum is:

to support its learners to become:

> - *ambitious, capable learners, ready to learn throughout their lives*
> - *enterprising, creative contributors, ready to play a full part in life and work*
> - *ethical, informed citizens of Wales and the world*
> - *healthy, confident individuals, ready to lead fulfilling lives as valued members of society*
>
> (Education Wales, 2025)

A first step, then, in evaluating a school's curriculum intent might be to ask the following questions:

- What is the school's vision for the curriculum?
- Is the intent comprehensive, and does it cover all the required elements?
- Who formulated that vision and how widely is it owned?
- What processes does the school have for involving stakeholders?
- What are the principles and goals underlying the curriculum?
- What is distinctive about the offer?

Curriculum content

A helpful definition of curriculum can be found in Education Scotland's *Curriculum for Excellence* (2008, p. 20):

> *The curriculum is the totality of experiences which are planned for children and young people through their education, wherever they are being educated. It includes the ethos and life of the school as a community; curriculum areas and subjects; interdisciplinary learning; and opportunities for personal achievement.*

The curriculum adviser might well ask the following of a school's curriculum offer:

- Does the content of the curriculum align with the overarching vision and principles in the statement of intent?
- Does it meet statutory requirements and pay due regard to non-statutory guidance?
- Is the curriculum sufficiently broad and balanced in each phase?
- How do curriculum areas work collaboratively to support curriculum delivery and coherence?
- How effectively does the use of curriculum time support the intent?
- How does the curriculum accommodate the needs of different students?
- Is the curriculum meeting its aims in terms of student outcomes, mindful of 'recognised' measures of success?

Curriculum affordability and sustainability

A key element of curriculum design relates to the affordability and value for money of a proposed curriculum offer. In England, for some years now, the central government has invested in a system called integrated curriculum and financial planning (ICFP). This is not a new idea, and it is not a silver bullet for times of financial hardship; it is, however, a systematic formal process, using a relatively simple set of metrics to inform discussion and planning, as illustrated in Figure 10.1.

Stage 1: Accurate student number projections

Use all available data to ensure that plans are based on a realistic prediction of student numbers within the school for at least the next three years; considering historic admission and retention trends, local demographics, any planned new housing developments and historic patterns of internal turbulence (leavers and arrivals in the middle of a school year).

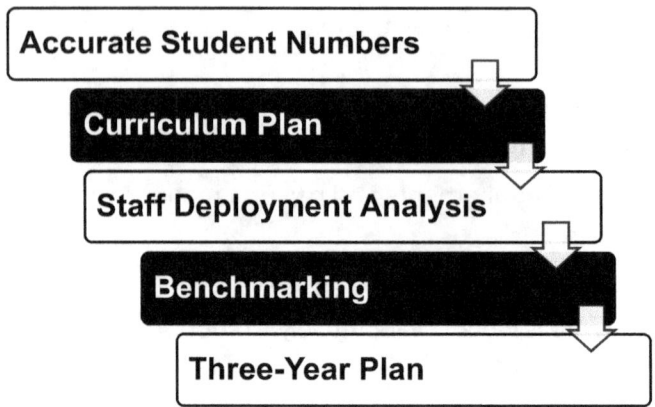

Figure 10.1 The five stages of integrated curriculum and financial planning

Stage 2: Constructing the curriculum plan

Produce a three-year curriculum plan that sets out exactly how many lessons and how many staff will be needed in each year group to deliver the curriculum content. Many schools still work on a year-to-year basis in their planning, but this can store up significant problems in the years ahead. The three-year plan is especially important when a particular admission group, for example, in a reception class in a primary school or in a secondary school with a sixth form, is well below previous averages or when a school is proposing to make significant changes to its historic curriculum offer.

Either of these scenarios can have a significant impact on staffing numbers and specialisms going forward. While, inevitably, forecasting funding levels and staffing costs ahead of time is an imprecise science, it is vital to the planning process that historical budgetary trends are used as a basis to estimate the impact of curriculum delivery models well in advance.

Stage 3: The staff deployment analysis

Conduct a staff deployment analysis on the curriculum plan to establish certain key metrics: teacher contact ratio, cost per lesson, average class size, pupil/teacher ratio, average teacher cost, leadership costs and curriculum bonus. Examples of this methodology can be found in the weblinks at the end of this chapter.

At this stage, the most important questions are:

- Is the curriculum plan affordable?
- How many teachers and other staff do we need?
- What is the contact ratio for teachers across the school?
- What percentage of the school's budget is spent on teaching and leadership?
- Is the distribution of delivery costs equitable across different phases?
- How many teachers and other staff can we afford?
- Are group sizes viable and realistic?
- Are we deploying staff efficiently?

The staff deployment analysis (SDA) is the most important stage of the ICFP process. It compares the cost of delivery in each phase or year group or course or subject with the income from student-led funding sources. One simple spreadsheet can reveal major discrepancies and anomalies between income and expenditure. Recent examples where SDAs have been applied include: one secondary school where the cost of curriculum delivery in the sixth form (ages 16–19) was, on average, costing £1000 more per student than the school received in funding per capita; one multi-academy trust of ten academies where the average contact ratio for teaching staff across the trust ranged from 62% to 78%. In both cases, governors were unaware of these anomalies.

The staff deployment analysis is, therefore, an invaluable tool for the adviser supporting a school and its governance in evaluating the affordability of a proposed curriculum plan, for example, the viability of class sizes in different phases, staffing costs in sixth form provision or optional courses, in-class support costs in a primary school, teacher contact ratios, leadership costs and so on.

Stage 4: Benchmarking

Benchmark the key metrics against other schools or groups of schools to compare relative expenditure in similar schools. While benchmarking as a process has its limitations and comes with some health warnings since all schools work in unique contexts, the process is designed to give leaders and governors a focus for discussion and decision-making.

Benchmarking expenditure can help lock a school into a cycle of continuous improvement and develop a culture where it is easier to question the norm and make changes. It should not be used solely to focus on reducing costs but also to improve the quality and impact of a school's provision, deploying resource where it is needed most.

Stage 5: The three-year ICFP analysis

Produce an ICFP analysis for at least the next three years. This process inevitably involves some informed crystal ball gazing, but it is important for leaders to project their best estimates of income and expenditure, including staffing costs, over a three-year period in order to arrive at the best possible indication of the impact of any changes in the medium term.

Conclusion

Supporting schools with curriculum design and review is a major area of focus for the education adviser. We hope this chapter will provide the adviser with a route map to guide the process, beginning with the vision, principles and goals of the statement of intent; scrutinising the strategies and content of the curriculum offer; and finally, evaluating the viability, value for money and sustainability of the model.

This process allows a school or a group of schools to maximise their resources, to target their provision where it is most needed and to improve the quality of the curriculum and outcomes for all learners.

Further reading

DfE England (2019, last updated in 2025) *Integrated Curriculum and Financial Planning (ICFP)*. Online at: https://www.gov.uk/guidance/integrated-curriculum-and-financial-planning-icfp. (Accessed on 24/04/25).

 References

Education Wales (2020, last updated 2025) *Curriculum for Wales: Designing Your Curriculum*. Online at: https://hwb.gov.wales/curriculum-for-wales/designing-your-curriculum/. (Accessed on 23/08/25).

The Scottish Government (2008) *Curriculum for Excellence: Building the Curriculum 3 – a Framework for Learning & Teaching*. Online at: https://education.gov.scot/documents/btc3.pdf. (Accessed on 24/04/25)

11 A perspective on recruiting an effective senior leadership team

ROISIN HARBINSON

Key learning

- Short-term effectiveness will not be sustainable if longer-term strategic approaches are not established.

- An effective senior leadership team should be unique to the school it serves.

- Moral and ethical leadership is crucial.

AoEA criteria

- Criterion 21: Understands the PESTLE drivers for change

- Criterion 23: Is able to link vision, policy, strategy, plans, goals and ambitions to long-term requirements and immediate needs

- Criterion 24: Links the job design and people development to strategic requirements

- Criterion 27: Is able to assess the context for organisational improvement

Introduction

In an ideal world, a principal would have a 'dream team' at the school leadership level. In the real world, more often than not, a leadership team is inherited and may fall short of that vision. We all have a tendency to judge a team against our ideas and beliefs of what 'effective' looks like. This immediately places limitations on our expectations and restricts our estimation of how a team could perform, evolve and transform with the right support, coaching and mentoring. In measuring the team against an idealised version, principals often perceive more limitations than are warranted. Still, the principal has a professional responsibility to develop and work with the team to bring about the best possible outcomes for children. In the short-term, gaps in the team need to be addressed to operationally manage the school efficiently, but the gaps also need to be considered within a longer-term improvement strategy. Davies (2006, p. 17) summarises this succinctly:

> *Short term effectiveness will not be sustainable if longer-term strategic approaches are not established. Schools will not be able to deploy longer-term strategy if short-term ineffectiveness drives the school into crisis.*

As a senior education adviser, I have the privilege of working with a range of senior leadership teams, all operating within unique settings in terms of finance and buildings, admissions, socio-economic background, special educational needs, language barriers, human resources and links with their community. Notably, the leadership models in the schools and the roles and responsibilities of the leadership team do not have the same level of diversity. It is apparent that the needs of the school, immediate and future, as articulated in the strategic plan, are not always aligned to the leadership model. The tendency to adhere to a traditional, conservative structure takes precedence over a structure that meets the immediate needs and strategic goals of the school.

Consider:

- How the management structure in your school differs from others?
- Why and how is it different?
- Why is it not different? Have we evidence to support this choice?
- What needs to change to drive learning and improvement in your unique context?

This chapter is designed to promote reflection and discussion about aspects of the school that need to be considered when recruiting an effective leadership team to serve the needs of the individual school.

So, what does an effective leadership team look like?

The main domains of leadership in a school can be categorised into leading ethos, leading improvement and leading learning. All capacity-building strategies should fall into one of the three categories. In this way, not only will the context of the school be improved, but it will be changed to enable a sustainable future for the children the school serves.

Leading ethos

It is a privilege to be part of a leadership team, but such privilege comes with a high level of responsibility. In schools, leadership teams are more than managerial efficiency. They shape the heart of the school, and their conduct and interactions with others are measured against the values and shared vision of the school. This has a powerful impact on the climate and context for school improvement. If the leadership team demonstrates compassion, care and respect, it boosts overall staff morale and leads to positivity in the school, which, ultimately, impacts on the children the school serves. Students are more likely to thrive in environments where the adults model positive, respectful relationships. It follows that leaders need to work within a moral framework, demonstrate and espouse the values of the school and communicate those to others. The image of the 'servant leader' emerges; Greenleaf's leadership team is one that is about lifting others to achieve greatness together. Consequently, a leadership team should be comprised of people who lead with moral and ethical behaviour and are aligned to the vision of the school. This is an essential backdrop for any 'dream team'.

Undoubtedly, it is a challenging task to develop morals and ethics in a leadership team. However, a focus must continually be placed on developing team aptitudes and personal attributes in the core values of commitment, respect, integrity, equality and service. The team will model the leader's behaviour, either consciously or unconsciously and the importance of spending time integrating new members into a leadership team with a clear focus on servant leadership, values and vision will be time well spent and an investment in the realisation of the strategic goals of the school. Despite the changing contexts of the school, there will be a moral compass to lead the way.

Consider:

- Does the leadership team display servant leadership?
- To what extent do the core beliefs and values of the school underpin the induction programme for new leaders?
- How are team aptitudes and personal attributes in the core values of commitment, respect, integrity, equality and service developed in the school's leadership team?

Leading learning and leading improvement

Leading learning and leading improvement are inextricably linked. Schools are learning organisations, and to be effective, the leadership team need to be the leaders of learning. There is a need to engage in research to be fully informed by the most up-to-date guidance and best practice to bring about improvements in learning. Hargreaves (2008) refers to the 4 deeps:

- Deep leadership;
- Deep support;
- Deep experience;
- Deep learning.

'Deep leadership' means to develop a culture and structures to promote improvement, best practice in self-evaluation, quality assurance and effective communication. Deep leadership needs to be driven by the leadership team and their roles and responsibilities assessed as to how they can contribute to and build on the other three 'deeps': 'Deep support' at leadership/system level to close achievement gaps; 'Deep experience' at leadership/system level to inspire and engage learners; and 'Deep learning' at classroom level to drive improvement.

To achieve such depths, there is a continual need to support and develop a leadership team via experience, coaching, modelling, mentoring and aligning their professional development needs and training to the strategic plan of the school. Thus, moving the structure and roles of the leadership team beyond superficial change to support more profound, systematic improvements.

It is vital that the principal and governors have a clear understanding of the school's strategic goals and can validate that the goals are firmly rooted in the values and ethos of the school. Thus, gaps in the current leadership structure – either in roles or responsibilities – can be identified and the current structure can be judged as to how effectively it meets the needs of the children the school serves. This will ensure that shorter-term effectiveness is complemented with a longer-term effective strategy.

Consider:

- To what extent does our culture promote improvement?
- Does our current structure (roles and responsibilities) enable deep learning?
- How does the leadership development programme prioritise and deepen learning?
- Is greater emphasis placed on teaching strategies and techniques to deeply support our student population and to bring about deep learning?
- Is the professional learning programme reflective of our deep experience of what our students require to overcome barriers to learning?

A senior structure to lead ethos, learning and improvement is not only shaped by the unique context of the school but also by the fact that the school exists within the wider social context of society. External factors need to be considered to develop a vivid vision and strategic direction for the school.

The PESTLE model can be used to analyse the external macro-environmental factors that can impact the school and is a useful tool as a driver for change, as Table 11.1 illustrates.

As a diagnostic tool, the PESTLE model will enable deep, rich and fruitful discussion at governor level to ensure the four 'deeps' are currently met, can be sustained in the future and can be clearly

Table 11.1 PESTLE impact on leadership focus

Area	Examples	Role/Responsibility for:
Political	Shared campus etc.	Deep leadership
	Government policy/decision making	Deep learning
		Deep support
	Curriculum changes	Deep experience
	Change of governance	
	Dealing with adverse publicity	
Economic	Economic – managing budgets/school and departmental/funding opportunities for the school	Deep leadership
		Deep learning
	Funding for extra-curriculum	Deep support
	Catchment area of the school – is there low income/unemployment and limited resources at home?	Deep experience
	Labour market information – national and international (curriculum review)	
Social	Diversity of intake	Deep leadership
	Need for nurturing facilities	Deep learning
	Free school meals (FSM)	Deep support
	Co-educational changes	Deep experience
	Demographic shifts	
	Cultural trends	
	Societal problems – mental health, substance abuse, etc.	
	Remote learning and skills needed	

→

Technological	Online learning platforms	Deep leadership
	Cybersecurity	Deep learning
	Digital platforms	Deep support
	New management systems/recording	Deep experience
	PR tools used – social media	
Legal	Safeguarding	Deep leadership
	Positive behaviour	Deep learning
	Admissions criteria	Deep support
	Recruitment and selection	Deep experience
	Health and safety	
	Safety online	
	Contractual considerations – support staff, etc.	
Environmental	New building/refurbishments/facilities in surrounding area/safety on and off buses/school entrance and exit.	Deep leadership
		Deep learning
	Green initiatives	Deep support
	Adapting to new road structures/climate-related issues	Deep experience

linked to roles and responsibilities at senior leadership level. Potential barriers can be anticipated and innovative, creative structures discussed to ensure the school has a resilient, sustainable leadership structure.

Some questions following the use of PESTLE may well emerge:

- Is the curriculum fit for purpose?
- Are there any gaps in provision?

- How does the curriculum align with the labour market?
- Is there value for money, for instance, in terms of class sizes?
- Are there any gaps/is there any duplication in the current staffing structure?
- Are there aspects of the staffing structure that no longer serve a purpose?
- Is the structure meeting the strategic needs of the school?
- Is the staffing structure fit for purpose?
- What areas of staff professional learning need to be addressed?
- Is there sharing of good practice?
- Is communication effective?
- Is the school a learning community?
- What leadership competences need to be developed further:
  - applying knowledge and understanding?
  - working with others?
  - solving problems?
  - communicating effectively?
  - what aptitudes and personal attributes in core values of care, compassion, commitment, respect, integrity, equality and service need to be developed?

How is the school performing, in terms of its:

- academic performance?
- inspectorate recommendations?
- admissions numbers?
- attendance and punctuality?
- students with special educational needs?
- students on free school meals?
- leavers' destinations?

- comparison to benchmark data?
- suspensions/exclusions?

Does the school leadership team have:

- an in-depth knowledge of the school in terms of outcomes for learners; standards attained; quality of provision; quality of the curriculum; effectiveness of guidance and support; effectiveness and impact of planning, teaching and assessment?
- self-evaluation for improvement at the core and integral to each individual's work?
- a shared culture of self-evaluation?
- an understanding of how their daily operational tasks fit into the longer-term strategy of the school?
- ability to inspire and influence others?
- an effective contribution to the whole-school development plan?
- high expectations for pupils?
- high standards for self and others?
- the ability to develop teams and individuals?
- the confidence to share leadership and delegate effectively?
- the ability to address underperformance?
- the ability to problem-solve?

With a comprehensive evaluation, an assessment of the context for school improvement can be judiciously assessed and weighted against the needs of a senior leadership team. The leadership team can be linked to the vision of the school both in the short term, to address immediate needs and, simultaneously, to support the vision's trajectory. Roles and responsibilities can be aligned to the strategic requirements and training needs of leaders aligned to the strategic goals of the school.

Conclusion

The educational landscape is becoming increasingly complex with many challenges facing leadership teams; the need for effective relationships have never been more avid. Senior leadership teams are on a voyage together, and before they set sail, they need a moral compass to address the storms ahead and a well-mapped route in the form of the strategic plan. The voyage may be long, so building relationships is crucial. By honouring the dignity and equality of those whose life we touch and by not placing limitations on the group, the journey should end at the destination we plan – or maybe somewhere even more exciting.

Further reading

Fullan, M. (2014) *The Principal: Three Keys to Maximising Impact*. San Francisco: Jossey-Bass.

Kirtman, L. (2013) *Leadership and Teams: The Missing Piece of the Education Reform Puzzle*. London: Pearson.

Spears, L. (1998) *Insights on Leadership: Service, Stewardship, Spirit, and Servant-leadership*. New York: Wiley.

References

Davies, B. (2006) *Leading the Strategically Focused School: Success and Sustainability*. London: Sage Publications.

Hargreaves, D. H. (2008) *The Deeps in Action*. London: Specialist Schools and Academies Trust.

12 Advising schools in areas of significant, socio-economic disadvantage

SIAN SMITH

Key learning

- School improvement is always a challenging task, but when combined with additional external pressures such as those found in areas of significant socio-economic disadvantage, it can feel like you are climbing a mountain in slippers!

- Leaders may encounter various challenges for which they require support. There are simple but effective advisory strategies that will support advisers and leaders to understand the issues and address them. These include:
    - understanding the context and create a shared understanding to form successful relationships between advisers and school leaders and school leaders and their stakeholders.
    - ensuring that evidence not assumptions inform decisions.
    - developing a roadmap using a school improvement plan and a shared vision with clear priorities and milestones, understood and known by all to create the start of school improvement.
    - helping leaders find and grow the people and give frequent and genuine feedback.

AoEA criteria

Criterion 22: Critically evaluates the design of the curriculum or educational offer

Criterion 23: Is able to link vision, policy, strategy, plans, goals and ambitions to long-term requirements and immediate needs

Criterion 24: Links the job design and people development to strategic requirements

Introduction

High-quality education should not be dependent upon the circumstances of a child's birth, sometimes referred to as a 'postcode lottery'. This belief has framed all my work, as a teacher, a headteacher and in my role as a teaching and learning adviser. My professional experiences have largely been within relatively impoverished communities in England.

I view school improvement here as a gold coin. On one side, you have 'achievement' and, on the other, you have 'readiness to learn'. The skill of leaders in these settings is recognising that for every pupil, the coin might be weighted differently and to respond accordingly. Success in these settings is when everyone, not just the leaders, does this too!

I am going to explore how educational advisers can support leaders to achieve just that, based on my direct experiences. Firstly, by framing *why* some communities face greater socio-economic challenges and their impact on the expectations for educational success. Then, I describe some of the strategies I employ: the *what* and the *how* of successful advisory work in these schools.

The 'why'

The Joseph Rowntree Foundation report *UK Poverty 2025* (Section 2) records that 3 out of every 10 pupils live in relative poverty. There is a wealth of evidence pointing to the causal relationship between poverty and a range of educational outcomes and potential for lifelong impact on individuals or groups across generations. Evidence points to higher probabilities of barriers to accessing resources, restricted opportunities and poorer standards of living. It can also lead to social exclusion, through isolation or marginalisation from mainstream society.

Leaders working in these communities are faced with dealing with the impact of wider societal factors such as housing instability; uneven parental engagement; and families experiencing poor physical, emotional and mental health. The lottery of circumstance is further exacerbated by uneven funding formulas. While some schools may receive additional funding, it is rarely sufficient.

While all schools face challenges, arguably the pressure of expectation can be felt most acutely in schools in areas of significant socio-economic disadvantage. Leaders know that they have to successfully address these challenges and influence children to succeed against the odds. Additionally, when standards are too low or variable and there are external accountability pressures, then the institutional stakes are also high.

Advisory strategies: the 'what' and the 'how'

Supporting the identification of priorities and strategy

Marc Rowland, a recognised national specialist in addressing educational disadvantage, argues that educational settings must correctly assess the barriers and not make assumptions about what they are. It is important that advisers are aware of strategies to support leaders to do just this. One example I have used with leaders is the *HIAS Tackling Educational Disadvantaged Toolkit* (HIAS, 2023). Using this tool, we review the school's practice through four different lenses focusing on: whole school culture and engagement; access, equality and strong foundations; expectations, pitch and response; and collaboration, dialogue and behaviours. *The Education Endowment Foundation Guide to the Pupil Premium* (2023) is another useful guide to signpost or work through with school leaders, as it has a wealth of research-based evidence to provoke discussion and suggest possible solutions.

Many of our schools face an overwhelming pressure for change and an overload of policy initiatives. With the best of intentions, they try and do everything and may end up by doing nothing well. Focusing on and prioritising school improvement planning and effective monitoring and evaluation strategies can be problematic when there may be multiple areas to address.

Michael Fullan (2001) argues that there are five core components of effective leadership for change: moral purpose, understanding change, relationship-building, knowledge creation and sharing and coherence-making. Analysing these key areas with leaders enables them to identify their vision as well as the non-negotiables that form the basis of agreed expectations. This builds the foundations of a school improvement strategy.

School improvement is a finely nuanced process, but I believe there are five key advisory approaches that culminate in a strategic plan that drives improvement. Without a plan, we don't have a strategic roadmap, and without a roadmap, we can't align all stakeholders around a common vision and shared responsibility. In my experience, the key steps to working effectively as an adviser are:

1. Build the relationship.
2. Understand the challenges and ensure that there is a shared 'truth'.
3. Agree the direction and share the plan.
4. Develop the people, including the ones you have and the ones you need to deliver the plan.
5. Evaluate the impact by asking have we achieved or are we closer to achieving our new 'normal' and revise, renew and repeat.

Building the advisory relationship

Effective advisers first establish relationships with the leaders with whom they are working. This involves facilitating supportive interactions with active listening, focusing on understanding their message and not responding based on assumptions. Show genuine interest, ask clarifying questions, paraphrase and reflect upon what you have heard and defer judgement. It does not mean that you agree with all their assumptions and beliefs, but it does mean that they have felt heard. For example, in one setting with which I have worked, the leaders had labelled themselves as the 'Naughty School' because they had been told they needed support. I helped them to reflect on their ambitions and persuaded them that additional support would be the extra weight they could use to tip the scales in their favour to achieve their aspirations. In another setting, I challenged leaders to move their focus from seeing Special Educational Needs and Disabilities numbers as a reason for their low standards to how they were addressing their needs. Using the national data to contextualise and supplying examples of how inclusive classroom practice was being implemented in other local and national settings provided a balance of challenge and solution-focused thinking.

Agreeing to the shared truths

As experienced educational professionals, we know that schools in areas of significant, socio-economic disadvantage face particular barriers, but these barriers are not exactly the same in all settings. It is, therefore, important that we come to a shared understanding with leaders of what the current context is, based on concrete evidence, not just assumptions.

There are several strategies one can use to create a shared 'truth'. For example, Lewin's force field analysis is an approach whereby you understand and manage change through identifying and analysing the forces that can either promote or hinder the change. By clearly identifying the desired goal or change and the associated driving and restraining forces, you can develop strategic plans to overcome obstacles and achieve desired aims.

Agreeing the direction and sharing the plan

Professor David Hopkins in his article *'Unleashing Greatness – A Strategy for School Improvement'* (2022) illustrates this through what he terms a 'school improvement pathway' (Hopkins, 2022, p. 16). He believes that there are five improvement dimensions that emerge along the school improvement continuum:

- curriculum;
- teaching;
- learning;
- assessment/data and accountability;
- leadership.

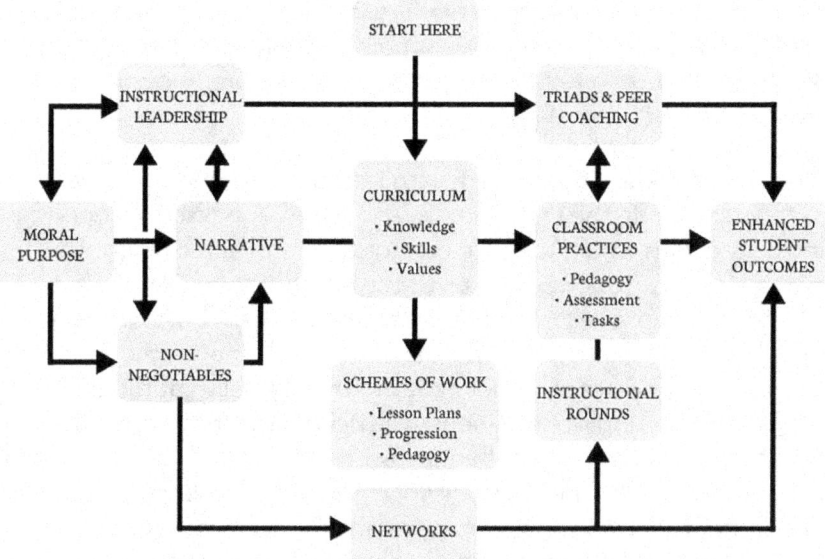

Figure 12.1 *Unleashing Greatness: An Interactive Model* (Hopkins, 2022)

The pathway, illustrated in Figure 12.1, also assists us in posing a series of questions. Hopkins argues that any school can use this pathway at any point in time, to reflect the context in which they work. I would argue that in the case of struggling schools in areas of significant, socio-economic disadvantage, it works best to start with the moral purpose/vision and creation of the non-negotiables to ensure that all stakeholders understand and sign up to both the journey and route map in front of them.

Support the development of people

Once a shared vision and aim is created, it is important that it is known by all as well as their role in achieving it. This requires leaders to not only articulate the vision but also to empower individuals to achieve it.

With teacher recruitment a challenge in the United Kingdom, it is not difficult to understand why schools in areas of significant, socio-economic disadvantage find it difficult to recruit the staff they need. Leaders can be faced with appointing someone because they fill a role rather than fulfil a role. We must, therefore, support leaders to grow the staff they need.

Education advisers should work with leaders to decide what type of leadership style they need to use and when. Too often, leaders find a style with which they are comfortable and fail to recognise that leadership is about using all the styles at different times and in different contexts. Some of the greatest success I have had is through helping leaders to read the room and behave accordingly. For example, one headteacher believed that by being autocratic, things were getting done. When we reviewed the impact, it was evident that middle leaders had followed a tick list of actions without understanding why these were important or the desired impact. This meant that there was no buy-in from any of the staff and changes were only superficial. I coached the headteacher to become more transformational and build a shared understanding and purpose, which meant that middle leaders could hold people to account to ensure that changes became embedded. I have also found that a focus on supporting greater teacher collaboration creates a sense of shared ambition and success.

Focus on feedback

Not only do leaders have to communicate a compelling vision to all, but they also must put systems and processes in place that support staff to achieve this vision. This involves ensuring that all staff know the role they have to play, have the appropriate continuous professional development to achieve it and are given appropriate feedback including genuine praise at different monitoring and evaluation points. Advisers need to support their leaders at all levels to do this, especially taking time to evaluate impact rather than just monitoring that something has been done.

Conclusion

Although one could argue that all schools face similar challenges, schools in challenging socio-economic circumstances face more, more often. Skilled education advisers support school leaders to be sensitive to, but not constrained by, their context. They enable leaders to actively mediate and moderate within a set of core values and practices which transcend from 'what else can you expect from our context' to 'there are no limits to what we can achieve'. This is true of teachers, too. It's not enough for teachers of the disadvantaged have a desire for improvement: they need to have a 'bucketful' of knowledge and expertise too. They should also strive to collaborate with other schools experiencing similar challenges to provide opportunities for joint problem-solving, enable the pursuit of shared goals and support collaborative professional learning, but that's another chapter!

 Further reading

Education and Endowment Fund (EEF) (2023) *The Education Endowment Foundation Guide to the Pupil Premium*. Online at: The EEF Guide to the Pupil Premium|EEF. (Accessed on 29/04/25).

Education Policy Institute (2024) *Annual Report*. Online at: Annual Report 2024 – Education Policy Institute. (Accessed on 06/05/25).

Roland, M. (2017) *Learning Without Labels: Improving Outcomes for Vulnerable Pupils*. Woodbridge, England: John Catt Educational Limited.

Roland, M. (2021) *Addressing Educational Disadvantage in Schools and Colleges*. Woodbridge, England: John Catt Educational Limited.

References

Fullan, M. (2001) *Leading in a Culture of Change*. San Francisco: Jossey Bass Wiley.

Hampshire Inspection and Advisory Support (HIAS) (2023) *Tackling Educational Disadvantage*. Online at: Tackling Educational Disadvantage (TED): Building Blocks for Excellence Overview. (Accessed on 06/05/25).

Hopkins, D. (2022) Unleashing greatness – A strategy for school improvement. *AEL*, 42(3), Lead Article.

Joseph Rowntree Foundation (2025) *UK Poverty 2025*. Online at: UK Poverty 2025: The essential guide to understanding poverty in the UK|Joseph Rowntree Foundation. (Accessed on 23/08/25).

13 The responsibilities of governance in ensuring a sustained, strategic focus on organisational development

EMMA KNIGHTS OBE

Key learning

- The governing board should set a vision and a strategic direction which ensures the organisation's development and sustainability.
- The organisation's strategy needs to be communicated well, annually reviewed with stakeholders, and focus the work of both the board and the senior leadership of the organisation.
- A healthy culture is essential for ensuring that the strategy can be delivered well.

AoEA criteria

- Criterion 21: Understands the PESTLE drivers for change
- Criterion 23: Is able to link vision, policy, strategy, plans, goals and ambitions to long-term requirements and immediate needs
- Criterion 27: Is able to assess the context for organisational improvement

Introduction

Our schools and academy trusts exist to provide the best possible education for their pupils. That is their mission; therefore, each organisation needs to develop their ability to deliver this in their context, adapting to changes in the community and broader society around them.

Any education adviser commissioned to work with a school or a trust on its development will need to engage from the outset with the governing board which exists to ensure the organisation is delivering their mission.

Research by Professor Toby Greany for the Department of Education (DfE, 2018) has shown that there are five areas to consider for sustainable school improvement or organisational development of trusts:

- vision, values, strategy and culture;
- people, learning, capacity and deployment of leaders;
- assessment, curriculum and pedagogy;
- quality assurance and accountability;
- a sustainable learning organisation with access to effective practice and expertise.

Securing an organisation's strategy and culture across a group of schools will set the foundation for those other four elements necessary for learning and improvement, providing for development which can be sustained over the years, rather than changing as senior leaders move on. That first area is one of the core functions of the governing boards of both standalone schools and multi-academy trusts (MATs). The other three are as follows and as developed more fully in Book 3 in the AoEA Education Adviser Series, *Advising on Governance in Education*:

1. Ensuring clarity of vision, ethos, culture and strategic direction for the organisation;
2. Holding the executive leaders to account for the educational performance of the school and its pupils and for the performance management of staff;
3. Overseeing the financial performance of the organisation and making sure its money is well spent;
4. Ensuring the voices of stakeholders are heard.

Working with only one academy within a MAT cannot be approached in the same holistic way; its development is affected by the trust's approach, and in turn, it should contribute to the development of the MAT and its other schools. Ideally the whole MAT needs to be considered in terms of school development as the academies are part of the same organisation. In addition, academy level governance works differently with the board of trustees specifying a delegated role. In this chapter, I am assuming that the adviser is working with either a standalone school, whether maintained or a single academy trust, or with a MAT on its strategy for organisational development.

Setting the strategic direction

Each trust or standalone school should have a strategy for the organisation with a small number of strategic priorities. That strategy is one of the first things an adviser would need to see at the outset of a new piece of work and to make an assessment – first is it a strategy at all? How was it arrived at? Does it truly represent the priorities the lead executive is pursuing across the organisation? This should be the key document shaping the organisation's development.

Fifteen years ago, being strategic was generally thought of as 'not being operational'. There were self-evaluation processes which resulted in school improvement or school development plans (SIP/SDP), but they tended to be lengthy operational plans. Although they were presented by the headteacher to governors as part of a crowded agenda, they were not in any way co-created. A board should be aware that such a management plan exists or what alternative management process is being used, but to go through a plan line by line is not a good use of a board's time. Instead, that progress check is the business of the headteacher or the chief executive. The lead executive might better report on progress by exception using red, amber, green (RAG) ratings. The main focus of the board is to discern and support the addressing of priorities against the strategy.

Time and space should be made, ideally in the summer term, to hold a strategy session for both the board and the school or trust leadership. There is simply not the time needed for the strategic and 'generative mindset' in regular business meetings, and an external facilitator can be used to underline the change of mode and spirit. Leaving these important deliberations until September is likely to mean they don't get enough reflection in the hurly-burly of the new school year.

Strategy sessions should take a very different format from regular board meetings with far fewer papers and open discussions with everyone participating and stakeholder input heard and welcomed. In a MAT, local governors can be included alongside trustees, even though it is the trust board which will sign off on the developed strategy. The environment outside the school/trust and future trends need be considered, for example, using a political, economic, social, technological, legal, environmental (PESTLE) analysis. Debate can be had as to what best drives value and success for pupils.

The National Governance Association in collaboration with National Association of Headteachers (NAHT) and Association of School and College Leaders (ASCL) publishes *Being Strategic*, a guide to strategy development for those leading and governing in schools and MATs. It covers how strategic priorities are identified, resourced and monitored and gives information on vision-setting, self-evaluation and risk assessment. It should provide a framework for governing boards and leaders to refer to if they are unfamiliar with the process or want to share information with staff or local governors within a MAT before an annual conference or 'away day' when the strategy is to be reviewed.

Key steps in the annual strategic cycle

Step one: where are we now?

Carry out an evaluation – it is entirely up to the school/trust how it sets out its evaluation, but it should give as accurate position as possible as to how well the school/trust and its pupils are currently performing.

Review against last year's strategy priorities (assuming you had them). Be realistic and honest when determining how much progress was achieved.

Step two: what might be coming up next?

Look at potential external changes. Strengths, weaknesses, opportunities, threats (SWOT) and PESTLE analyses can be useful. Risk analysis should form part of that evaluation. This discussion should be more wide-ranging than that seen at a standard board meeting. All ideas should be welcome, though more exploration is likely to be needed for new and innovative considerations. As with all board decisions, good judgement should be exercised after good debates.

Step three: confirm the vision

The vision should, in a few sentences, describe what pupils will leave the school(s) knowing, being and having done. The vision should be to continuously improve and make the experience of the school the very best it can be for pupils, parents and staff. Projecting forward a few years, are there any new goals you want the school/trust and its pupils to have achieved? There is no need to rewrite the vision annually, but it is good practice to review it.

Step four: what are the obstacles in the way of achieving our vision?

Using both the current performance and the future opportunities and risks, identify the challenges and potential obstacles to achieving the vision. Concentrate on overcoming those that are most important and likely to have the most impact on the children's learning or your other identified goals.

Step five: the board agrees the strategic priorities for the coming period

The strategy should include a small number of key priorities – often five or six – which help achieve the vision. These need to be ambitious but also achievable with focused attention and determination. They also need to take account of what stakeholders told you was of most importance to them. A strategy can be high level for a number of years, usually three or five, but with more specific objectives for the coming school year.

Step six: how can we ensure our resources support the achievement of the priorities?

Identify the resources you have and tailor them to help achieve the vision and the priorities, not the other way around. This might include a review of the staffing strategy.

Step seven: how will you know whether you are achieving the vision?

The strategy document needs to include what success looks like for each priority and what evidence is needed to measure progress. This should result in measures of what you value, and they won't all be quantitative. Even though the strategy is for a three-to-five year period, progress will be evaluated throughout the year. The lead executive's reports to board meetings should be based on the measures set out in the strategy, and the priorities should also inform their appraisal objectives.

The board can decide whether to assign one or two governors/trustees to monitor each priority, sometimes termed a 'link' role. This must not detract from the whole board being responsible for organisational development, but it can help to increase the knowledge of some members. Whether strategy links are beneficial depends, in part, on the board's committee structure.

If other unexpected issues arise, flexibility may be required. The board can consider whether there is now an additional immediate priority, but if this is the case, thought needs to be given to why this wasn't identified during the review process. Ensuring the organisation's work focuses on the agreed priorities should have the benefit of reducing distraction, including the noise of some seemingly urgent current events.

Step eight: communicate the strategy

The executive should make sure this happens and that stakeholders understand why decisions were made and how their input was used. With trusts, the strategy should also be presented at the annual general meeting. There needs to be buy-in from as many people as possible.

Step nine: back to the beginning and where are we now?

Culture of the organisation

The board together with the leadership have to create the right culture for the strategy to succeed, and an adviser will need to ascertain if this is the case:

> *An effective governing body promotes its vision, culture and ethos across the whole school and ensures that is reflected in its policies and its practices.*
> (DfE, 2024b, *Maintained schools governance guide*, section 2.1)
>
> *Culture: The board and executive leadership team anchor the academy trust's strategy in the needs of its schools, the communities they serve and the wider educational system in line with its charitable objects. The board, accounting officer and executive leadership team create a culture of ethical leadership.*
> (DfE, 2024a, *Academy trust governance guide*, section 1)

The culture of an organisation – 'the way things get done around here' – should flow from its values and ethos. It may have developed over many years and might not be perceived in the same way by everyone. The culture will often be affected by a change of senior leadership, but if it truly comes from the school/trust's values and ethos, it should stand the test of time.

The board should set and safeguard an ethos of high expectations for everyone in the school community. This includes high expectations for the behaviour, progress and attainment of all pupils and for the conduct and professionalism of staff and board members themselves. Figure 13.1 helps to illustrate this.

'A strategy that is at odds with a company's culture is doomed. Culture trumps strategy every time – culture eats strategy for breakfast'. Attributed to Peter Drucker and popularised in 2006 by Mark Fields, president of Ford Motor Company. You may well have heard this much-quoted axiom at a leadership conference: it does not render strategies redundant but emphasises the need for a culture that supports the strategy, and vice versa.

The governance board and an adviser must understand the organisation's culture and climate – the way things feel. To do that they need to hear from stakeholders, in particular the staff. It is imperative that boards understand staff morale. This can be overlooked by governors and trustees not wanting to confuse the lines of management; however, it is increasingly important given sector-wide challenges with staff workload and retention. An adviser may need to support this happening well.

All schools and trusts should embrace being a learning organisation. This should be a primary concern of the board, championing professional learning at all levels, from the board to non-teaching staff, and ensuring there is the time, resource and expertise dedicated to doing this well.

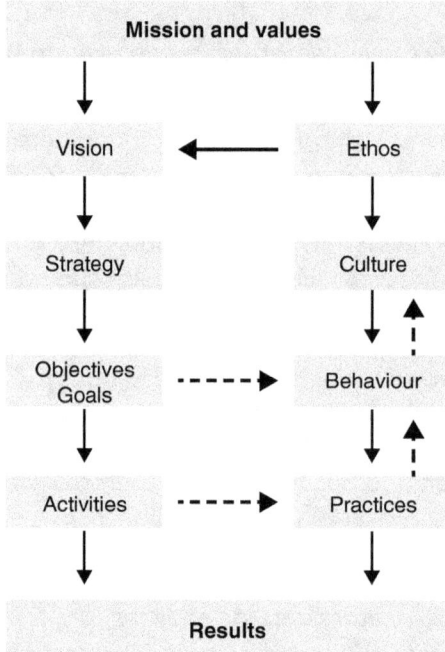

Figure 13.1 Developing a strategy and culture which work together

Conclusion

Approximately 4 in 10 of the commissions referred to National Leaders of Governance (NLGs) from 2021 to 2023 showed organisations struggling to determine a meaningful vision and strategy. Remember these were schools and trusts which the regulator, the Department for Education (DfE) or local authority had concerns about, but it demonstrated that there is still some way to go before this fundamental tenet of organisational development is fully understood and embedded across the sector.

Education is a people business, and developing people will lead to organisational development. This should be obvious, but there was considerable time when the latest scheme for school improvement was promoted rather than an organisation considering the needs of its staff. Even so, not every school or trust has a people strategy. This may well be an area an adviser needs to highlight or probe further.

 Further reading

National Governance Association (2024) *Chair's Handbook, NGA, 10th Edition*. Online at: https://www.nga.org.uk/knowledge-centre/the-chairs-handbook-paperback/. (Accessed on 09/05/25).

National Governance Association (2025) *Being Strategic for Single Schools, NGA, NAHT & ASCL*. Online at: https://www.nga.org.uk/knowledge-centre/strategic-guide-boards-leaders. (Accessed on 22/04/25).

National Governance Association (2025) *Being Strategic for MATs: NGA, NAHT & ASCL*. Online at: https://www.nga.org.uk/knowledge-centre/strategic-guide-boards-leaders. (Accessed on 22/04/25).

National Governance Association (2023c) *Governing a Multi Academy Trust: A Handbook for Trustees, NGA*. Online at: www.nga.org.uk/knowledge-centre/welcome-to-a-multi-academy-trust/. (Accessed on 09/05/25).

National Governance Association (2023d) *Charting the Course to Good Governance: Common Challenges, NGA*. Online at: www.nga.org.uk/knowledge-centre/external-reviews-good-governance/. (Accessed on 09/05/25).

National Governance Association (2024) *Growing Good Governance: Exploring the Legacy of the National Leaders of Governance Programme, NGA*. Online at: https://www.nga.org.uk/media/i04pcfdu/growing-good-governance-20240624.pdf. (Accessed on 09/05/25).

References

Department for Education (December 2018) *Sustainable Improvement in Multi-School Groups, Research Report* by Toby Greany, UCL Institute of Education/University of Nottingham.

Department for Education (March 2024a) *Academy Trust Governance Guide*. Guidance on Strategic Leadership and the Governance of Academy Trusts. Online at: https://www.gov.uk/guidance/-governance-in-academy-trusts. (Accessed on 09/05/25).

Department for Education (March 2024b) *Maintained Schools Governance Guide*. Guidance on the strategic Leadership and Governance of Local Authority Maintained Schools. Online at: https://www.gov.uk/guidance/governance-in-maintained-schools. (Accessed on 09/05/25).

Part 3
The impact of leadership on performance

14 The importance of ethical leadership in organisational development

CAROLYN ROBERTS

Key learning

- The Framework for Ethical Leadership in Education (FELE) can support quality decision-making in schools.

- The seven 'virtues' or personal characteristics of ethical leadership offer a framework for leaders to reflect.

- Advisers can use questions informed by the FELE as part of their conversations about organisational development.

AoEA criteria

- Criterion 23: Is able to link vision, policy, strategy, plans, goals and ambitions to long-term requirements and immediate needs

- Criterion 24: Links the job design, people development and strategic requirements

- Criterion 25: Is able to analyse management procedures and systems

- Criterion 26: Is able to apply a variety of measurements of success and performance indicators

- Criterion 27: Is able to assess the context for organisational improvement

Introduction

School leaders make decisions: small ones, big ones, immediate ones and long-term ones. What to do about the roadworks outside the school gate, how to deal with a vitriolic parent or an underperforming teacher, resolving a serious behaviour issue or designing a curriculum. Decision-making can be trivial or life-changing, collegial or lonely. Most decisions are made in a context of unavoidable ambiguity. How can leaders take confidence in their own choices?

There are perhaps 25,000 headteachers or principals in the English school system. Leaders' autonomy is said to be highly prized, but the dominance of accountability systems has skewed leaders' approaches to problem-solving and decision-making. Should they act as they believe to be right, or should they follow instructions? What should they do about issues upon which accountability measures appear to be silent, or contradictory? If they fear for their jobs, how can they reflect calmly and rationally upon the problems they face?

Decision-making is challenging in England in 2025. Teachers are scarce and leaving the profession. Money is tight, and many schools simply cannot balance their budgets. Successive chief inspectors have downplayed and underestimated the effect that their (simplistic, because also underfunded) judgements have on leaders' behaviour, including the design of schools' curricula. There is an upsurge in children with special educational needs, widespread parental anger and significant behaviour management challenges.

Given the breadth of these daily issues, it might not be surprising that many leaders are tempted to seek safe solutions, prioritising accountability over professional judgement.

It is at this point that education advisers can play a unique role in leaders' decision-making, unpicking the foundations and processes of a leader's thinking and reflecting with them on their motivations.

The Framework for Ethical Leadership in Education

The *Framework for Ethical Leadership in Education* (FELE) was developed in 2018 by a group of English educational leaders and thinkers, including unions, churches and the inspectorate convened by the Association of School and College Leaders (ASCL). It aimed to offer school leaders a set of agreed, broad and timeless principles upon which to base decisions. The Commission's report that launched the Framework was called *Navigating the educational moral maze*. It is now promoted and enabled by another high-level group, the Ethical Leadership Alliance, under the leadership of the Chartered College of Teaching.

The Framework begins with the UK's seven 'Principles of Public Life' (often referred to as 'The Nolan Principles'), launched for the guidance of public office-holders in 1994. As touched on in the previous book in this series, these are its *values*:

1. *Selflessness*: leaders should act solely in the interest of children and young people.
2. *Integrity*: leaders must avoid placing themselves under any obligation to people or organisations that might try inappropriately to influence them in their work. Before acting and taking decisions, they must declare and resolve openly any perceived conflict of interest and relationships.
3. *Objectivity*: leaders must act and take decisions impartially and fairly, using the best evidence and without discrimination or bias. Leaders should be dispassionate, exercising judgement and analysis for the good of children and young people.
4. *Accountability*: leaders are accountable to the public for their decisions and actions and must submit themselves to the scrutiny necessary to ensure this is the case.
5. *Openness*: leaders should expect to act and take decisions in an open and transparent manner. Information should not be withheld from scrutiny unless there are clear and lawful reasons for so doing.
6. *Honesty*: leaders should be truthful.
7. *Leadership*: leaders should exhibit these principles in their own behaviour. They should actively promote and robustly support the principles and be willing to challenge poor behaviour wherever it occurs. Leaders include both those who are paid to lead schools and colleges and those who volunteer to govern them.

Schools and colleges serve children and young people and help them grow into fulfilled and valued citizens. As role models for the young, how we behave as leaders is as important as what we do. Leaders should show leadership through the following personal characteristics or *virtues*:

1. *Trust*: leaders are trustworthy and reliable. We hold trust on behalf of children and should be beyond reproach. We are honest about our motivations.

2. *Wisdom*: leaders use experience, knowledge and insight. We demonstrate moderation and self-awareness. We act calmly and rationally. We serve our schools and colleges with propriety and good sense.
3. *Kindness*: leaders demonstrate respect, generosity of spirit, understanding and good temper. We give difficult messages humanely where conflict is unavoidable.
4. *Justice*: leaders are fair and work for the good of all children. We seek to enable all young people to lead useful, happy and fulfilling lives.
5. *Service*: leaders are conscientious and dutiful. We demonstrate humility and self-control, supporting the structures, conventions and rules which safeguard quality. Our actions should protect high-quality education.
6. *Courage*: leaders work courageously in the best interests of children and young people. We protect their safety and their right to a broad, effective and creative education. We hold one another to account courageously.
7. *Optimism*: leaders are positive and encouraging. Despite difficulties and pressures, we are developing excellent education to change the world for the better.

The Framework is not a leadership manual. It requires personal, professional reflection before a leader makes any decision. It requires a commitment to consistent self-analytical thinking and a level of scepticism about off-the-peg or oven-ready solutions.

An example

An adviser is supporting a leader thinking about curriculum change in KS3 and 4, rooted in underachievement in maths. They are discussing a range of actions:

- formal monitoring of the subject leader, with clear achievement targets;
- moving to setting from mixed-ability teaching (or vice versa);

- buying a readymade programme of study for teachers to follow;
- increasing the amount of maths in KS3, by reducing practical subjects;
- embedding more examination practice and methodology in KS3 and 4.

The leader is not certain whether to implement any or all of them but is determined to take action. None of the actions listed is unusual in school, but many of them reflect the principal's vision and motivation, and all of them involve ethical choices. The skilled adviser takes time to investigate this. Is she worried about maths because the results are low and will affect the school's reputation? Is it because children are not getting the knowledge and skills they need for life? Is it because maths results are particularly important to inspectors? How does she articulate the purpose of education? Is it measured by examination results or are examination results a partial measure of its purpose?

Looking at the proposals, the adviser will then move to assess the context for action in pursuit of improvement. Using the Framework for Ethical Leadership in Education, an adviser can begin a deep discussion with the principal.

1. *Selflessness*: which actions are in the best interests of children and young people?
2. *Integrity*: is there a conflict, such as a family member with an off-the-peg maths programme?
3. *Objectivity*: what evidence base is she using for class organisation decisions?
4. *Accountability*: which decisions could best withstand scrutiny?
5. *Openness*: who is or will be involved in the decision? Are governors or trustees involved?
6. *Honesty*: is the principal's description the whole truth of the matter. Is there anything else? Has she been honest about her concerns with the subject leader? What view does she hold of pedagogy? Does she believe that teachers need very tight guidance?
7. *Leadership*: what kind of leadership is being expressed?

a. *Trust*: what will serve the children best? Are her maths teachers subject experts? Would a bought-in curriculum affect or compromise their self-understanding? Are they struggling to teach out of subject and would they, therefore, welcome a bought-in scheme?

b. *Wisdom*: how has her experience, knowledge and insight helped? Are the proposed decisions rational? Which will be most effective? Which may have unintended consequences? Is there a likely replacement for the head of maths if that becomes necessary?

c. *Kindness*: what support has the head of maths received? how will she deal with hardworking maths colleagues who have been diligent in trying to improve outcomes?

d. *Justice*: will all children be served by proposed changes, or just a subset, such as the most able? What effect will change have on struggling or disadvantaged children? What would curriculum narrowing do for younger children's potential?

e. *Service*: what is the value of a broad and balanced curriculum, and of Key Stage 3? Are her proposed actions scalable? If every school behaved this way, would the system be the better for it?

f. *Courage*: are the decisions required in order to remove complacency or poor practice and, therefore, serve children better? Will the head of maths need support to achieve this?

g. *Optimism*: what are the likely best results of change? How will they develop excellent education to change the world for the better?

Why this is important

Schools are where society looks after its young until they are old enough to take up the mantle of adult citizenship. During schooling, they deserve to be given adult role models of the very highest standard. Such adults think very carefully before they act, weighing the likely consequences of each action for the good of the children in their school and the strength of the education system they serve.

Ethical disciplines become habitual. A leader who becomes used to considering the FELE is able to apply it quickly and instinctively. Embedded in institutional processes, it builds coherence and offers a calm, shared language for making and understanding decisions. Used by advisers, it builds a bridge between them and school leaders, the broader system and the children, upon whose understanding of ethical behaviour in the future we all depend.

Conclusion

Most organisational development decisions are made in situations of unavoidable ambiguity. The systematic use of the FELE between adviser and leader can enable calm, mature reflection and help the leader develop confidence in their own decision-making. This not only reduces stress but enables the leader to step back from educational 'panic' and short-term solutions.

Using the FELE encourages a leader to align and embody vision, ethos and decision-making for the long-term benefit of the organisation and the wider system. The wider such thinking spreads, the stronger our schools.

Further reading

Ethical Leadership Commission (2019) *Navigating the Educational Moral Maze*. Online at: Navigating-the-educational-moral-maze.pdf. (Accessed on 06/05/25).

National Governance Association (NGA) (2025) *Ethical Leadership in 300 Pathfinder Schools*. Online at: Search Results Page | National Governance Association. (Accessed on 06/05/25).

Roberts, C. (2019) *Ethical Leadership for a Better Education System*. London: Routledge.

15 Assessing the impact of leadership on the Context for Organisational Improvement (COI)

LES WALTON CBE, PETER PARISH AND IAN LANE

Key learning

- Leaders have a significant influence on the Context for Organisational Improvement (COI) and its impact on learner outcomes.

- Working with leaders, education advisers have a key role to play in evaluating and assessing the COI.

- COI provides us with the means, through a staff lens, of identifying key strengths and areas of working practice in need of further improvement.

- COI focuses on lead indicators rather than lag indicators, which can be measured and monitored for their impact, assisting leaders in proactively developing the organisation.

AoEA criteria

- Criterion 23: Is able to link vision, policy, strategy, plans, goals and ambitions to long-term requirements and immediate needs

- Criterion 26: Is able to apply a variety of measurements of success and performance indicators

- Criterion 27: Is able to assess the Context for Organisational Improvement

Introduction

Organisational context significantly influences workplace culture and performance, particularly in educational settings such as schools and trusts. Leadership helps to shape this context, affecting staff morale, teamwork, and overall efficiency. A positive organisational context fosters collaboration and motivation, whereas a negative one can lead to disengagement and inefficiency.

Recognising this, the Association of Education Advisers (AoEA) has developed an approach rooted in Herzberg's motivation-hygiene theory (1968) and Burke-Litwin's performance and change model (1992). This adapted framework assesses and seeks to enhance the organisational environment through seven key dimensions:

- *Vision*: clarity of organisational goals and direction;
- *Policy*: effectiveness of rules, procedures, and administrative systems;
- *Responsibility*: delegation of authority and accountability;
- *Achievement*: emphasis on performance improvement and goal-setting;
- *Recognition*: incentives and rewards for performance;
- *Relationships*: trust, teamwork, and collaboration;
- *Sustainability*: ability to anticipate, adapt, and respond to change.

By analysing these dimensions, leadership teams can identify areas for improvement and foster a working environment that supports professional growth and organisational success. The education adviser can have a key role to play in assisting in this process.

Conducting a Context for Organisational Improvement (COI) analysis

A structured self-assessment questionnaire is used to measure organisational context. Staff members evaluate their perception of the current environment and their ideal vision for its future. A 40-statement questionnaire covers the 7 dimensions, with responses averaged and displayed graphically to highlight discrepancies.

The results may be presented as a block diagram or similar format, as illustrated in Figure 15.1. Significant gaps between the current and

Receiving and Understanding Data on the Context for Organisational Improvement Survey

Figure 15.1 Analysing the Context for Organisational Improvement

desired states indicate areas requiring attention. For example, low scores in 'vision' may suggest a lack of clarity regarding goals or roles.

Leadership teams should engage in discussions with staff to explore solutions by considering questions such as:

- Are organisational goals, policies, and procedures clearly communicated?
- Do staff have access to strategic plans in an accessible format?
- Are responsibilities well-defined and understood?
- What suggestions do staff have for improving clarity and effectiveness?

Through open discussions, leaders gain valuable insights and can implement meaningful changes that enhance organisational cohesion and effectiveness. Advisers, too, can help to facilitate this process. Table 15.1, covering each of the dimensions, can be used to assist in such an analysis.

Table 15.1 Exploring with staff the Context for Organisational Improvement

Context dimensions	Key issues and questions
Policy (and administration) *The perception staff have about the policies and administration within the organisation are that they support people to do their jobs and to take the initiative.*	• Are there burdensome systems of administration? • Are there unnecessary rules and procedures? • Do people feel they have to fight against unreasonable constraints? • Do senior staff place more emphasis on getting the job done or on following the rules? • Is there too much paperwork to complete?
Responsibility *The perception that staff have clear delegated, authority and that professional advancement is improved by taking responsibility and seeking creative solutions.*	• Are important tasks delegated to staff? • Are individuals encouraged to take initiative without always checking with a supervisor? • Are individuals encouraged to take calculated risks, based on their own judgement? • Are individuals allowed the opportunity to experience the success or failure of their own efforts?
Achievement *The perception staff have about the importance placed on continuous improvement of professional conduct and achievement and that very high expectations of achievement are established*	• Do senior leaders place emphasis on performance and continuous improvement of performance? • Are realistic but challenging goals set on the job? • Are there opportunities for individual participation in goal-setting and planning at appropriate times? • Do individuals receive information and feedback regarding goal accomplishment?

⟶

Recognition (and Remuneration) *The degree to which staff perceive that great importance is placed on identifying and incentivising good performance and that career advancement and recognition is based on the quality of work that people do.*	• In general, do rewards seem to outweigh punishments? • Are available rewards tied directly to performance quality? • Does the head offer valued recognition of top performers? • Does good performance lead to increased opportunities for individual growth?
Vision (and Planning) *The staff are clear about the vision of the organisation and how plans and systems are clearly linked to the vision. They are also clear about how they can contribute, as individuals, to the objectives of the organisation.*	• Do individuals have a clear idea of what is expected of them? • Do individuals know how they personally contribute to the mission? • Do individuals feel that work gets done in an orderly and timely fashion? • Are goals, policies, procedures, and lines of authority clearly articulated and understood?
Relationships *The perception that staff have a high level of trust, pride, and teamwork within the organisation and put in extra effort to ensure meetings and management systems work well.*	• Do individuals co-operate effectively to get the job done? • Are conflicts resolved effectively? • Do various groups co-ordinate their efforts effectively on tasks? • Do feelings of trust, pride, and organisational loyalty exist in the workplace?
Sustainability *The perception that the moral purpose of the organisation helps individuals to find meaning in their work, that change and sudden disruption is anticipated, responded and adapted to.*	• Does the moral purpose of the organisation help individuals find meaning in their work? • Is the organisation able to anticipate, respond, and adapt to change and sudden disruptions? • How effective are the mechanisms for addressing risk mitigation? • Does the organisation have strategies to support personal resilience?

The role of leadership in organisational improvement

Effective leadership is fundamental to a positive organisational context. Leaders influence all COI dimensions, from setting a clear vision to fostering recognition and teamwork. Strong leadership empowers employees, creating an environment where they feel valued and motivated.

The AoEA promotes systems' leadership, which focuses on removing barriers to improvement. Systems' leaders go beyond managing operations; they create environments where innovation, collaboration, and professional development thrive. By addressing organisational bottlenecks, leaders can drive sustainable improvements and create a culture where staff perform at their best.

Leadership evaluation should accompany a COI analysis to ensure management policies and systems align with organisational goals and working practice. Successful leaders actively listen to staff concerns, implement strategic changes, and foster an inclusive and supportive working environment.

The impact of leadership styles on organisational improvement

While it is not an absolute science, different leadership styles tend to have an impact on the seven key COI dimensions in the following ways:

- *Directive leadership*: task-focused, might positively impact on achievement and vision but negatively affect relationships and sustainability.
- *Visionary leadership*: tends to have strong positive impact across most areas, particularly in relation to enabling a shared understanding of the organisation's core purpose, policy, responsibility, and achievement.
- *Affiliative leadership*: strengthens relationships but may weaken policy and achievement if not counter-balanced.

- *Democratic leadership*: enhances relationships and responsibility but can slow decision-making and achievement.
- *Modelling leadership*: positively influences responsibility and relationships, but its impact on achievement tends to be mostly short-term.
- *Coaching leadership*: provides long- and short-term benefits across multiple areas, particularly vision, relationships, and sustainability.

A leadership impact diagram may be used to helpfully summarise the positive, negative, and variable effects on context dimensions, as illustrated in Figure 15.2.

COI and leadership analyses serve as a continuous improvement tool rather than a one-time assessment. Conducting these analyses regularly, such as at the start and end of the academic year, allows leadership teams to track progress and adjust strategies accordingly, in consultation

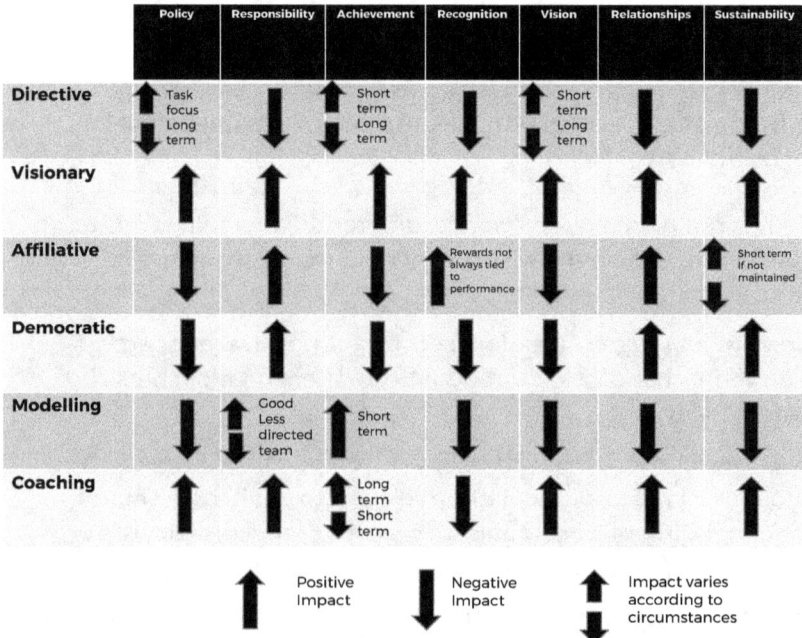

Figure 15.2 Impact of leadership styles on organisational context

with their staff. These analyses can also be used to benchmark results against other schools or across a group of schools, such as a trust, facilitating collaboration and learning from one another's practice.

Conclusion

A COI survey serves as a lead indicator, offering insights into the inner workings of an organisation's effectiveness. Unlike lag indicators, such as inspection outcomes or examination results, this lead indicator provides, across the full suite of 'context dimensions' proactive, predictive, and actionable insights in the 'now'.

Advantages of using lead indicators are that they:

- provide a proactive approach, enabling intervention in key areas of working practice before negative trends emerge;
- provide predictive insights, identifying early signs of future performance challenges or successes;
- focus on sustained high performance in working practice, encouraging continuous improvement rather than reactive fixes;
- give greater control, enabling leadership to directly influence factors within their organisation;
- provide timely feedback, offering 'real-time' data on the effectiveness of actions taken;
- provide a holistic perspective enabling evaluation inclusive of academic performance, staff morale and community engagement.

When the context dimensions within an organisation are rated high, staff experience greater autonomy, motivation, and organisational efficiency. Low ratings often indicate excessive bureaucracy, lack of accountability, and reduced morale. Addressing these dimensions holistically will help to ensure long-term, sustainable success. Leaders and advisers working with schools have a critical role to play in shaping this context for sustaining improvement. Periodic COI and leadership analyses, open discussions, and well-informed strategic actions and interventions enable organisations to create a thriving work environment where all feel empowered to make the difference.

References

Burke, W. W., & Litwin, G. H. (1992) A causal model of organizational performance and change. *Journal of Management*, 18(3). Online at: BurkeLitwin_ACausalModelofOrganizationalPerformance.pdf. (Accessed on 26/03/25).

Herzberg, F. (1968) *One More Time: How Do You Motivate Employees?* Harvard Business Review Classics, Harvard Business Review Press, 2008.

16 Empowering leaders through effective organisational development

MATTHEW HUMPHREYS

Key learning

- Organisational development is an ongoing and systematic process based on the building of habits which instil clarity of focus and enable continuous self-evaluation, meaningful change and improvement.

- The school improvement professional is well-placed to support effective and collaborative organisational development in a complex and ever-changing education system.

AoEA criteria

- Criterion 21: Understands the PESTLE drivers for change

- Criterion 22: Critically evaluates the design of the curriculum or educational offer

- Criterion 26. Is able to apply a variety of measurements of success and performance indicators

Introduction

I suspect you have had a similar experience of board games as my own. Initially, there is plenty of enthusiasm. However, once the box is opened, the challenge begins! Invariably, the rules of the game are so complex that it takes time to gain any sense of clarity. You feel your willingness to play swiftly slipping away. That is if you have managed to gather all the players, including the ultra-competitive one! Once all have a shared understanding of the rules, you then spend time ensuring all the necessary pieces are distributed. It takes considerable effort to even get to the starting point. Supporting effective organisational development has some notable parallels with this familiar routine.

Making sense of the changing rules of the game

Effective organisational development requires support for leaders to make sense of the rules.

When considering organisational development, we need to understand the driving forces behind any changes to practice and processes. One of the common drivers behind organisational development within the education system is wide-ranging reforms. Any reform within an education system presents both opportunities and challenges. Indeed, the breadth, scope, and pace of reform in Wales has provided plenty of both. For school leaders, the task of interpreting and implementing such change is no mean feat. For example, *Curriculum for Wales* is the flagship national education reform. As a purpose-driven curriculum, it presents highly aspirational intentions for pupils and greater autonomy for the teaching profession. So far, so good! However, the policy and guidance documentation presents school leaders with a huge challenge in just comprehending the rules of the game. Additionally, overarching school improvement policy performed a pivot from a heavy accountability focus to a more supportive approach. An opportunity to remove some of the unintended consequences of elevated levels of accountability has been welcomed. Then again, without familiar measures, how do we know how well we are doing? As a school improvement professional, it is vital to provide much needed clarity to assist leaders in developing an appropriate strategic response.

Equipping the key players

Effective organisational development requires key players to be fully equipped with a shared understanding of policy and any associated requirements.

One of the key advantages of a supportive approach to school improvement is that it enables the building of trust. For example, as a school improvement professional, it is possible to approach school leaders as a partner. The aim becomes to improve rather than to prove. This is foundational and has to be established before beginning to equip key players.

Accurately assessing barriers to organisational development is a key early step. This can be achieved through careful consideration of a range of first-hand evidence to build an accurate picture as to where the current successes and challenges lie. To ensure this process is robust and to build confidence, it is often necessary to work alongside colleagues in undertaking this part of the process. Not only does this provide additional intelligence and a critical voice, but it also serves as an illustration of the power of collaborative working.

Upon completion of any analysis, it is essential to communicate findings clearly and concisely to school leaders. Alongside this communication, there should be opportunities for leaders to access support in a range of forms. We will now consider the significant changes in Wales to illustrate this process.

In response to curriculum reform, common issues have arisen across many schools. Due to the complexity, volume and pace of reform, individual school leaders have been under significant pressure. This has presented a barrier to driving forward curriculum design aligned with the requirements of national policy. With this being so, it is vital to identify other 'key players' and equip them to support progress.

Key players look different in various contexts. The term could encompass senior leaders, middle leaders, or those with emerging leadership qualities. Whoever they may be, there is a need to provide clarity and distil key messages from policy to build shared understanding across an organisation. For example, in supporting key players across my school portfolio, clear distribution of roles and responsibilities has enabled each to play their part in responding to curriculum reform. Furthermore, they are equipped through targeted professional learning, coaching, and mentoring to develop expertise in curriculum design.

Bringing people together

Effective organisational development requires meaningful collaboration based on shared improvement priorities to build capacity.

If the empowering of leaders to drive organisational development begins with a shared understanding, it accelerates within collaborative structures. Working across multiple schools, organised into clusters, provides opportunities to develop meaningful collaboration. Current Welsh Government policy places increased emphasis on such an approach. The Government seeks to *'promote collaboration so that schools and settings are able to work together with increased ownership and with high trust'* (Welsh Government, 2020).

Effective organisational development requires the capacity to drive improvement at pace. This is a core strength of school-to-school working. Schools of all shapes and sizes are able to pool intelligence and provide a range of perspectives when dealing with shared priorities. For example, clusters of schools have benefitted from collaborating to build a shared understanding of curriculum progression. Having gained clarity as to the requirements of the policy, key players now have the benefit of designing a response through collaborative effort. A further benefit of collaborative discussions is the way in which less confident practitioners learn from colleagues and, as a result, formulate effective practice in their own context.

As the *Curriculum for Wales Framework* is a continuum for learners aged 3 to 16, it is essential for primary and secondary school colleagues to develop collaborative working relationships. Such collaboration enables the development of a progressive curriculum, which removes potential barriers to pupil progress. Collaborative groups of a smaller scale have proceeded to focus on specific areas of the curriculum and develop commonalities in content across school clusters. Furthermore, collaborations have not only considered what to teach but how to teach it. The work of the improvement professional to support this is vital.

An example of effective collaboration can be found in work carried out within a cluster of schools to strengthen independent learning. Developing the independence skills of pupils has been a common area to address and a prominent recommendation within the inspectorate's recent annual reports. As part of this agenda, pupils across Wales are required to demonstrate increasing effectiveness as learners. This includes the ability to self-assess their work and identify their next steps in learning. Furthermore, pupils are expected to develop the capability to analyse information and propose solutions to problems. This is the area of focus which our own collaborative looked to address in partnership.

Senior leaders supported colleagues to engage in collaborative working based on the understanding of the following key principles. Firstly, the focus for collaborative working would be informed by national policy. Additionally, evidence-informed practice would provide a foundation for discussion. Furthermore, practical solutions would be developed to support improvement in each school.

From the outset, key policy messages were shared such as the prominent place independent learning skills hold across *Curriculum for Wales*. Indeed, there are references to such skills throughout many aspects of *Curriculum for Wales* documentation (the Four Purposes, principles of progression, integral skills and pedagogical principles). Evidence-informed practice was drawn from the inspectorate's good practice case studies, the Education Endowment Foundation, and additional sources. The materials shared demonstrated the wide and varied ways in which pupils' independence skills could be enhanced. This included a focus on metacognition, effective use of feedback, providing choice in learning, and the acquisition of problem-solving skills.

Having built a shared understanding of policy requirements and effective practice, small-scale action research plans were created. One such piece of research involved teachers equipping pupils to build metacognitive skills into their learning. Pupils were encouraged to use simple set questions during the planning, monitoring, and evaluation of their learning. Pupils were empowered to seek and apply solutions to the problems they identified through their use of metacognitive questions.

As a result of this particular piece of action research, pupils have increased opportunities to develop independent learning skills. They demonstrate increasing understanding of their own learning and make choices as to how they achieve learning intention. These skills are in line with the aims of *Curriculum for Wales*. Additional benefits have been the growing clarity amongst teachers as to what constitutes true independent learning. Extra capacity for improvement has been achieved as well as the development of a culture of openness and partnership between schools. This is a clear departure from the previous policy which cultivated a closed culture under a heavy burden of accountability. Collaborative models emerging within the context of *Curriculum for Wales* have potential to successfully foster improved classroom practice.

Good outcomes follow quality practice

Measuring the impact of organisational development is more than just a numbers game. While quantitative data is informative, there is a rich vein of intelligence found through qualitative evidence. Aligning policy, people and practice is central to high-quality organisational development and sustainability.

In measuring success, it is important to consider how key players have successfully implemented effective practices. Within an education setting, this requires the careful consideration of a range of first-hand evidence. This allows consideration of the growing impact of leadership. Furthermore, the degree to which schools engage in evidence-informed practice and collaborative opportunities can provide a picture of emerging changes resulting from support. Early evidence, such as interim Estyn reports, suggests an increasing range of independent learning skills exhibited by pupils. Teachers provide greater choice as to resources pupils can select and use. Pupils have an increasing voice in influencing how and what they learn. Furthermore, pupils demonstrate a greater grasp of how the feedback process can be used to consolidate and extend their learning.

Success measures in Wales are increasingly qualitative rather than quantitative. This is due to the removal of many data-driven performance measures in the Welsh system. Ultimately, in seeking effective organisational change within schools, our focus is pupil outcomes. This means accessing a broad range of data through work scrutiny, pupil voice activities, lesson observations and learning walks, to name just a few. If organisational development has been successful, improved outcomes for learners will become clear across the evaluative activity which takes place.

Let us return to our previous examples. In developing successful organisational change in Wales, meeting the requirements of *Curriculum for Wales* required comprehensive organisational development. Where this was strong and effective, success was seen in an increasingly rich, deep and relevant curriculum. Pupils increasingly understood the purpose behind intended learning and demonstrated growth in their ability to connect and apply knowledge, skills and experiences. This is where we see the policy, clearly understood and applied, affecting the practice and, as a consequence, the outcomes.

Conclusion

Let us return to our board game. Once we have explained the rules, equipped the players and formed teams, we are all set. Similarly, we have seen that effective organisational development requires support for leaders to make sense of the rules. In addition, it requires key players to be fully equipped with a shared understanding of policy and any associated requirements. To further accelerate progress, there should be meaningful collaboration based on shared improvement priorities to build capacity. The role of the school improvement professional within this process is vital. It is incumbent on them to distil key messages and bring the right people together. Additionally, they are well-placed to provide access to appropriate support and resources. Crucially, the school improvement professional, working with a group of schools and aware of the dynamics and strengths at play, is in a position to broker beneficial collaborative working to support the process.

The educational reforms in Wales are complex. With this being the case, any organisational development requires careful evaluation and application of both strengths and further developmental needs. Organisational development is an ongoing evaluative and systematic process. It is also a collaborative learning process based on a shared understanding of how far we have come and what still needs to be done to continue to improve together.

Further reading

Evans, G. (2023) A new dawn or false hope? Exploring the early implementation of *Curriculum for Wales. Education Inquiry*, 1–15. Online at: https://doi.org/10.1080/20004508.2023.2297506. (Accessed on 07/02/25).

Smith, K. (2024) Reconceptualising curriculum in a new era of Welsh Education Wales. *Journal of Education*, 26(2), 54–71. Online at: https://doi.org/10.16922/wje.26.2.5. (Accessed on 07/02/25).

 References

Welsh Government (2020) *Curriculum for Wales: Implementation Plan* (under 'How do we get there, Roles and Responsiblities'). Online at: https://hwb.gov.wales/curriculum-for-wales/curriculum-for-wales-implementation-plan#page-wrapper. (Accessed on 07/02/25).

17 Enabling a structured approach to collaboration across a diverse system of schools in Northern Ireland

CATHERINE WEGWERMER MBE, HARRY GREER, DAMIAN EANNETTA AND JACKIE WALLACE

Key learning

- Effective collaboration requires an understanding of the diverse needs and contexts of schools.

- Structured frameworks and support systems are essential for successful partnership working.

- Leadership plays a crucial role in fostering a collaborative culture and sustaining partnerships.

- Continuous improvement and adaptability are key to maintaining effective collaboration.

AoEA criteria

- Criterion 22. Is able to evaluate critically the design of the curriculum or educational offer

- Criterion 23. Is able to link vision, mission, policy, strategy, resources, plans, goals and ambitions to long-term requirements and immediate needs

- Criterion 27. Can assess the impact of leadership on the context for organisational improvement

Introduction

In the ever-evolving landscape of education, collaboration among schools has emerged as a pivotal strategy for enhancing teaching and learning outcomes. The concept of school-to-school collaboration is gaining momentum across many highly developed education systems and is at the heart of successful school improvement. This chapter explores a structured approach to collaboration across a diverse system of schools, drawing on a project called *Pathways Into Partnership*, which supports primary and nursery schools in Northern Ireland in establishing professional learning communities (PLCs).

The importance of this advisory work and guidance lies in its potential to significantly enhance how teachers work and how pupils learn, ultimately leading to improved educational outcomes. By fostering a culture of collaboration, schools can share best practices, address common challenges, and leverage collective expertise to drive continuous improvement.

Building the foundations for the project

The *Pathways Into Partnership* initiative was designed to support primary and nursery schools on their collaborative journey and to potentially become part of a PLC. The intention underpinning this initiative was to create a flexible and adaptable framework that allows schools to set the pace and direction of their collaboration. Further envisaged outcomes included improved teaching and learning, enhanced professional development for teachers, and the establishment of sustainable and impactful partnerships. The purpose of this work was to research and design the guidance and develop the support mechanisms to realise the vision.

The initiative commenced with a school leaders' consultation in March 2021. Observations from this, along with the research and experience of the team, informed the development of a guidance booklet for schools. This became an important working manual stepping leaders through each of the stages of collaboration. A wide range of guidance, webinars for leaders and local authority staff, and teacher professional learning modules for use in schools were developed. These were further supported by professional learning events co-designed and facilitated by the AoEA. Local authority school improvement professionals (SIPs) worked alongside each partnership, and this developed into a strategic oversight group of the programme.

When launched, the initiative was offered to schools on a voluntary basis, thus giving them the autonomy to opt in as appropriate to their context. In March 2022, a cohort of 269 schools across the jurisdiction received seed funding to support the progression of their collaborative efforts.

Stages of collaboration

The framework, as outlined in Figure 17.1, is structured into five stages of collaboration, a preliminary stage followed by a further four stages. This framework allows schools to consider at a glance where they sit on the continuum of collaboration. It helps to frame their focus as they assess their unique starting point. This enables them to join a partnership at a stage appropriate to their own readiness and most relevant to them and to join with other settings who are well-placed to work effectively with them. Further, as the partnership progresses, review of the current stage of collaboration can be an agenda item that reminds, affirms, and guides the partnership.

Figure 17.2 builds on this and shows how each stage is stepped out. For each stage, it gives the participating school leaders clear actions to work towards – the 'how to' of collaboration and decisive outcomes. These provide the framework and the professional space for reflection and for open, equitable discussion. Through

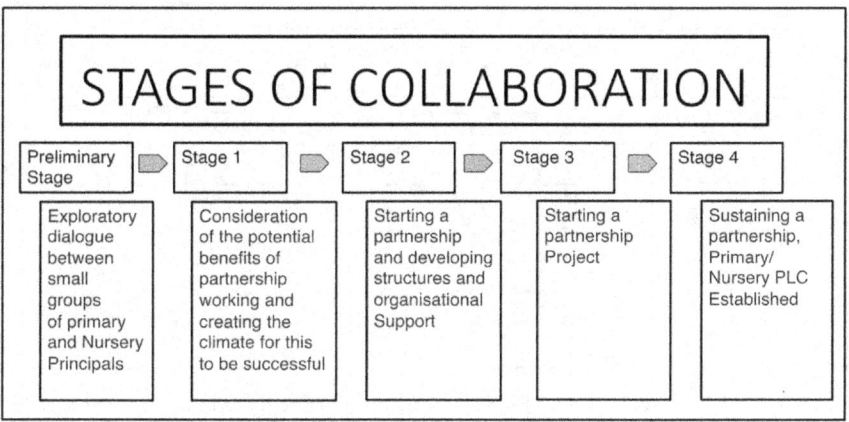

Figure 17.1 The stages of collaboration (Wegwermer et al., 2022, p. 8)

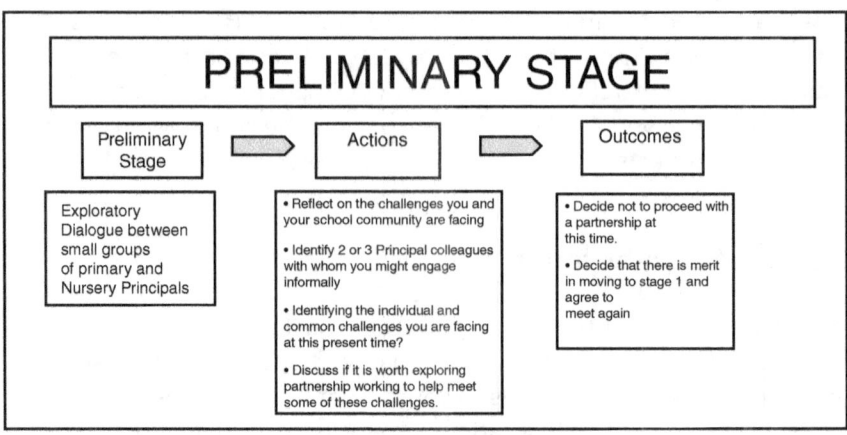
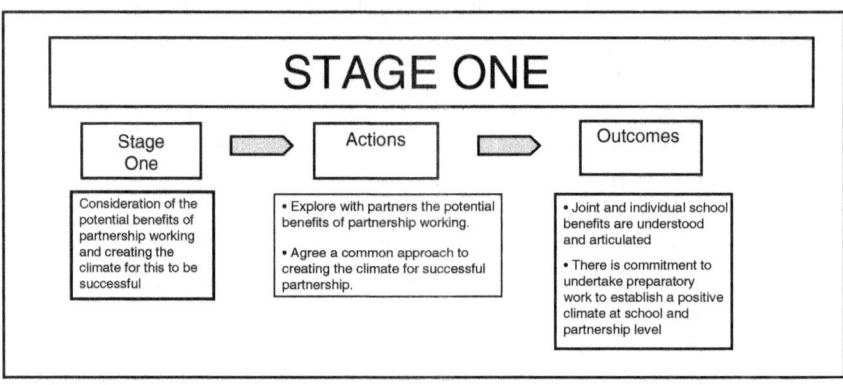
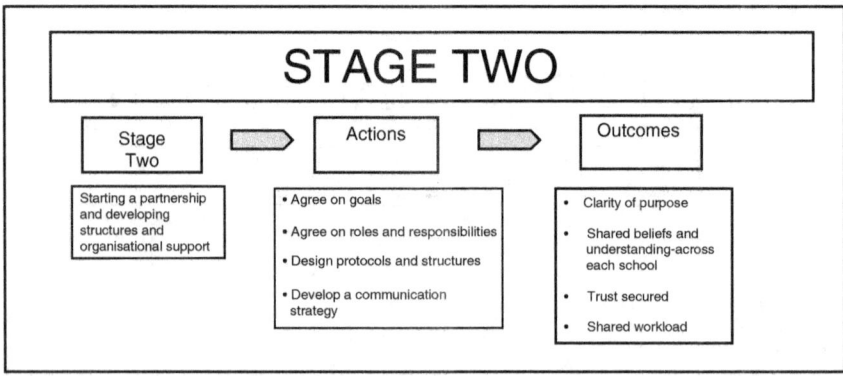

Figure 17.2 Possible actions and outcomes at each stage of collaboration (Wegwermer et al., 2022, pp. 9–20)

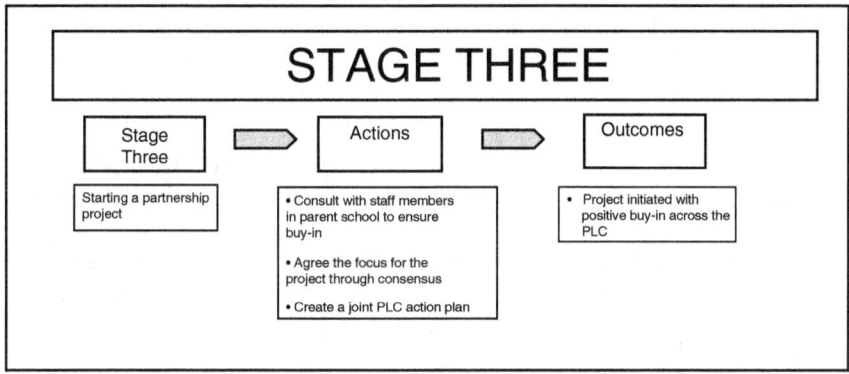

Figure 17.2 (Continued)

this, the partnership, often supported by their SIP, becomes clearer on where they sit on the continuum of collaboration, their unique and shared starting point, and their pathway towards a full and active partnership.

The Preliminary Stage affords school leaders the space to begin discussions about collaboration, especially where this is something new or different to their setting. Preliminary Stage actions and outcomes reflect the tentative nature of this stage. Schools and school leaders who are intentionally prioritising collaboration as something new can work comfortably here. Laying the foundations for successful partnership involves knowing who else is out there that you may already work well with and awareness that some of the challenges in your school are not unique to your school but mark a beginning towards potentially formalising already existing connections. School leaders can opt in or opt out based on these discussions and their informed position.

Stage 1 continues to lay the foundations for successful partnership. It moves into the benefits of collaboration as well as considering and creating the climate to work in partnership. School leaders discuss the benefits of partnership for their individual setting and for this collective. They agree on finer actions at school and at the partnership level that begin to formalise the relationship.

Stage 2 looks at building on structures within each partnering school and structures within the partnership itself. This brings structure to the steering team of the partnership. Here participants consider and agree more deeply on the purpose of this collaboration, its structures, and the roles and responsibilities of each member. They agree on shared expectations and communication mechanisms. These build on the clarity of conversation of the two previous stages. Everyone knows who is around the table, what they bring, and why they are working together.

Stage 3 identifies the partners' first collaborative project. By analysing the strengths and priorities coming forward from each participant, the partnership agrees on a focus that they each can buy into and that they can communicate and take action on as a priority within their own setting and together. They draw up, communicate, and make progress on a shared action plan. Their work from the earlier stages where they established the climate for partnership stands them in good stead at Stage 3. Here they really need that space to say what is working, what isn't working, and to understand why. Successful completion and review of the project consolidates Stage 3.

Stage 4 affirms that the partnership has successfully completed a project and is confident to review its own work and to continue to progress agreed projects together. When partnerships are working within Stage 4, they know and feel their professional autonomy and responsibility. They own the space of leading their school and co-leading the partnership and its work. They can evaluate the context of their school within the context of the partnership and express that clearly. They afford the same space to their partnership colleagues. Stage 4 consolidates the partnership as one of collaboration and shared responsibility for improvement. The partnership knows who is around and beyond the table, why they are working together, and what they have already achieved. They can conceive and enact sustained improvement for all the partnering schools and their communities.

Collaborative skills and behaviours

To have a truly collaborative partnership, everyone must have a voice, be on equal footing, and be able to contribute their abilities and skills to the work. The Pathways approach suggests the following collaborative skills and behaviours be nurtured to help develop the culture needed. Participants can consider the skills that they each bring. They can consider the collaborative behaviours they have already that they can further strengthen through collaboration. Table 17.1

Table 17.1 Collaborative skills and behaviours

Collaboration	
Skills	**Behaviours**
⇒ Open-mindedness ⇒ Communication ⇒ Co-ordination/Organisation ⇒ Long-term thinking ⇒ Adaptability ⇒ Debate ⇒ Co-operation ⇒ Assertiveness ⇒ Autonomy ⇒ Responsibility/Accountability ⇒ Emotional intelligence	⇒ Silo 'busting' ⇒ Building trust ⇒ Aligning body language ⇒ Promoting diversity ⇒ Sharpening 'soft' skills ⇒ Creating 'psychological safety' ⇒ Resilience ⇒ Not being offended easily ⇒ Not taking criticism personally ⇒ Being able to recognize and detach from strong emotions when needed ⇒ Curiosity
Using collaboration skills within a team may include:	
• Keeping communication open and never withholding information necessary to carry out tasks; • Reaching a consensus about goals and methods for completing projects or tasks; • Offering recognition of the contributions of others on your team, giving credit where credit is due; • Identifying obstacles and addressing problems co-operatively as they occur; • Placing group goals above personal satisfaction and/or recognition, especially if you're the leader; • Apologising and forgiving others for mistakes; holding a grudge or sabotaging the efforts of other team members destroy collaboration.	
Source: (Wegwermer et al., 2022, p. 7)	

referencing collaborative skills and behaviours is applicable at all stages as an individual point of reflection, of consolidation, and of refocus. It highlights some of the behaviours that, if not already there, further encourages individual participants to work in this way. As each individual becomes more aware and intentionally adopts the behaviours of effective teamwork, a culture of effective teamwork and collaboration is gently nurtured.

Impact and outcomes

The *Pathways Into Partnership* initiative has demonstrated significant success in fostering collaboration among schools. By June 2024, over 80% of primary and nursery schools were involved in the initiative and had received funding to support their collaborative work. Key success outcomes include:

- *Enhanced professional learning*. Teachers and school leaders have benefited from shared learning experiences, leading to improved teaching practices and professional growth. The initiative has provided opportunities for teachers to engage in collaborative enquiry, share practices which work well, and develop new skills. This has resulted in a more effective and confident workforce, better equipped to meet the diverse needs of their students.

- *Improved student outcomes*. Collaborative efforts have led to more effective teaching strategies, resulting in better student engagement and performance. Schools involved in the initiative have reported successes across a range of indicators including higher levels of student achievement, increased motivation, and improved attendance rates. By working together, schools have been able to identify and address common challenges, leading to more targeted and impactful interventions.

- *Sustainable partnerships*. Schools have established strong, trust-based relationships that support ongoing collaboration and continuous improvement. The initiative has fostered a culture of mutual support and shared responsibility, enabling schools to work together towards common goals. This has resulted in more resilient and adaptable partnerships, capable of sustaining long-term improvement efforts.

- *Leadership development*. School leaders have developed the skills and knowledge needed to foster a collaborative culture and drive school improvement. The initiative has provided opportunities for leaders to engage in professional development, share experiences, and learn from one another. This has resulted in more effective leadership practices, which are better equipped to navigate the complexities of the education system and drive meaningful change.

Conclusion

The *Pathways Into Partnership* initiative highlights the importance of a planned, structured, and co-facilitated approach to collaboration in education, an approach that everyone has access to. By providing a flexible framework, robust support systems, and a relatively small amount of funding, schools can effectively navigate partnership working, with increasing autonomy and ownership, and achieve meaningful outcomes relevant to their context.

Leadership plays a crucial role in fostering a culture where collaboration is key to sustaining continuous improvement. This work has supported participating school leaders in understanding the process of becoming a collaborative partnership. Moreover, it has strengthened an education system in becoming a collaborative partnership, developing skills and behaviours of all participants in themselves, in their settings, and in deepening the understanding of what we can improve together.

Further reading

Dufour, R., Dufour, R., Eaker, R., & Many, T. (2009) *Learning by Doing: A Handbook for Professional Learning Communities at Work.* Bloomington, IN: Solution Tree Press.

Elmore, R. (2002) *Bridging the Gap between Standards and Achievement: The Imperative for Professional Development in Education.* Washington, DC: Albert Shanker Institute.

Goldenberg, C. (2004) *Successful School Change: Creating Settings to Improve Teaching and Learning.* New York: Teachers College Press.

Harris, A., & Jones, M. (2010) *Professional Learning Communities in Action.* London: Leannta Press.

Lewis, C., & Andrews, D. (2004) *Lesson Study: A Handbook of Teacher-Led Instructional Change.* Philadelphia, PA: Research for Better Schools.

References

Wegwermer, C., Greer, H., Eannetta, D., & Wallace, J. (2022) *Pathways Into Partnership: Supporting the Development of Primary and Nursery Professional Learning Communities.* School Development Service, Education Authority Northern Ireland. Unpublished manuscript.

18 Building bridges: A case study in supporting 'deputes' to become headteachers

GRANT GILLIES

Key learning

- The numbers of applicants for headship nationally are in decline, with some regions struggling to fill vacancies.

- The continuum of professional learning often means that formal training for headship such as 'Into Headship' or the National Professional Qualification for Headship (NPQH) is at the wrong time in a leader's career, often overlapping with a first headship appointment.

- Deputy headteachers often feel confident dealing with operational aspects of headship but remain less so when it comes to the strategic aspects of the role, such as budgeting, recruitment, health and safety and formulating a vision for the whole school to lead sustainable change.

- This chapter offers insight into an adviser's role in designing a course to support 'depute' headteachers on their journey to headship with some evidence of impact and reflection on lessons learned.

AoEA criteria

Criterion 22: Critically evaluates the design of the curriculum or educational offer

Criterion 24: Links the job design and people development to strategic requirements

Criterion 27: Is able to assess the context for organisational improvement

Introduction

The landscape for leadership has changed around the world, and with it, the role of the headteacher has evolved as have expectations. Schools remain at the heart of communities, and their heads are often held to account for a wide range of societal challenges from failing academic standards to a huge increase in both diagnosed and undiagnosed additional support needs (ASN). It's a tough job that is, undoubtedly, an absolute privilege, so within this context of high stakes accountability with limited resource, who wants to be a headteacher? The answer is fewer and fewer people. The number of depute heads who want to take the 'leap' into headship is very small. While there is no nationally held data in relation to the success or otherwise of recruiting new headteachers to the role, the Association of Headteachers and Deputes in Scotland has produced some startling statistics. As one of the main professional bodies representing primary school leaders in Scotland, their annual workload survey provides a real insight into the leadership crisis in Scottish schools. When the survey started in 2016, 36% of deputes and 39% of primary school teachers who responded indicated that they were keen to become a headteacher. In 2024, those saying they were keen to become a headteacher had dropped to 15% of depute headteacher and 14% of primary teacher respondents, respectively. By implication, as many as 85% of depute heads currently in the role are not expressing the desire to become a headteacher. You can see why posts are being readvertised!

There is a very formal route into headship in Scotland, regardless of the sector. The *Into Headship* programme became mandatory for new headteachers in Scotland in 2015. This programme is designed to support aspiring headteachers and ensure they meet the *Standard for Headship* set by the General Teaching Council for Scotland (GTCS). The programme is similar in duration to the National Professional Qualification for Headship (NPQH) but delivered exclusively by teacher education institutions in Scotland. In the AHDS survey, 47% of those who indicated they were currently undertaking the programme were in acting or substantive headships, and an additional 28% across all those who had undertaken the programme reported having moved into an acting headship role whilst doing the course. In effect, this means almost half of the participants are balancing studying and headship, something all providers counsel against. Readiness for headship is in the interests of all in the teaching profession. Many demands are made on modern heads, involving a diverse range of skills, from business balancing to understanding parental rights and responsibilities. It is a fantastic job, and one I have loved in the six settings I have led. From inner city schools with high deprivation to fee paying British International Schools overseas, I have enjoyed every minute of my role. My family have adapted to the constant calls and 'spill over' from private life into professional life, attending and supporting all manner of wider school community events. It is a lifestyle and a choice I relish, as I say, a real privilege.

Context for change – a new course

Drawing on knowledge of supporting the *Into Headship* programme at national level and the Council of British International Schools (COBIS) *Programme for Aspiring Heads* internationally, I designed a course for deputy heads in Edinburgh across all schools. The course began as a pilot in January 2024 and targeted six to eight participants with a focus on practical support including financial, legal, and corporate elements.

Challenges and risks for the course

One of the first challenges was to persuade the local authority to allow me to work on helping to provide a solution for this growing problem. Working with our quality improvement manager (QIM), I reviewed the number of headship posts I had seen advertised and any information I could find nationally.

The identified shortfall in the number of applicants for headteacher posts in Edinburgh is linked to the shortfall in the number of people completing *Into Headship*, not least since completion of the programme is a mandatory requirement. In this cycle, we saw a shortfall of four. One in three posts are now readvertised, and I wanted to delve deeper into the root cause of the reluctance of leaders to become headteachers and what aspects I could influence for the better at corporate level across Edinburgh.

The case for action

It is arguably the enormity and multifaceted nature of the role that creates reluctance in potential candidates putting themselves forward for headship. With this in mind, I designed a course based on practical training and support to assist in developing our community of depute headteachers. The Local Authority has fully supported the course programme believing it will directly and positively impact on the challenge to recruit. The QIM was the main contact for the *Into Headship* course and perfectly poised to provide the coaching element in the first session. The course itself provided cross-developmental opportunities, through elevating specialists in their field to share their expertise but also in allaying fears and demystifying the role of headship for deputes, by 'breaking down' the constituent parts of the role and connecting participants with experts in key specialist areas so that the perceived role is not as overwhelming.

My own experience, too, has assisted in the development of this programme, from working as a headteacher for many years in a very challenging school with one in three pupils in abject poverty, to being principal of an independent school in Bucharest, Romania. I have completed the NPQH and National Professional Qualification for Executive Leadership (NPQEL) and have worked with the General Teaching Council for Scotland (GTCS) and Education Scotland (Ofsted equivalent). The breadth of this experience assists in an understanding of balancing the challenges of headship with the carefully managed leadership development for aspirant heads. Measuring readiness for headship is tricky as a starting point, but the pressures of becoming a new headteacher, combined with studying, risks diminishing the potential to recruit much needed new school leaders. The competencies laid out by the GTCS clearly outline demonstrable attributes, and *Into Headship* provides a network of very supportive colleagues passing through academic exploration of the role and introspection at an individual level. The *National Into Headship Programme Evaluation Report* (Education Scotland, 2022) highlighted various aspects that participants felt worked well, such as collegiate working, and the elements that could have been improved upon, most notably delivery methodology.

Course design

Initially, we envisaged recruiting 6 deputy headteachers with their headteachers as a pilot (12 in total). There are 112 schools in Edinburgh. The course we designed would serve as a practitioner-led enquiry, and I sought the opinions of colleagues to identify the barriers preventing depute headteachers from continuing their journey to becoming headteachers. We had to close the applications at 12 participants (twice the anticipated number), and it was instantly clear there was a need for a bridge to create more helpful steps between the depute headteacher and headteacher roles.

One of the greatest challenges would be to evidence the impact of our course programme. While applications in relation to *Into Headship* provides quantitative data, there would be a substantial time lag before we could measure the impact of any new course provision. I, therefore, focused on measurable aspiring leader confidence with 'pre', 'during', and 'post' course questionnaires as illustrated in Figures 18.1 and 18.2. Initial questionnaires also helped to inform course content.

Figure 18.1 Ranked areas of confidence in becoming a headteacher

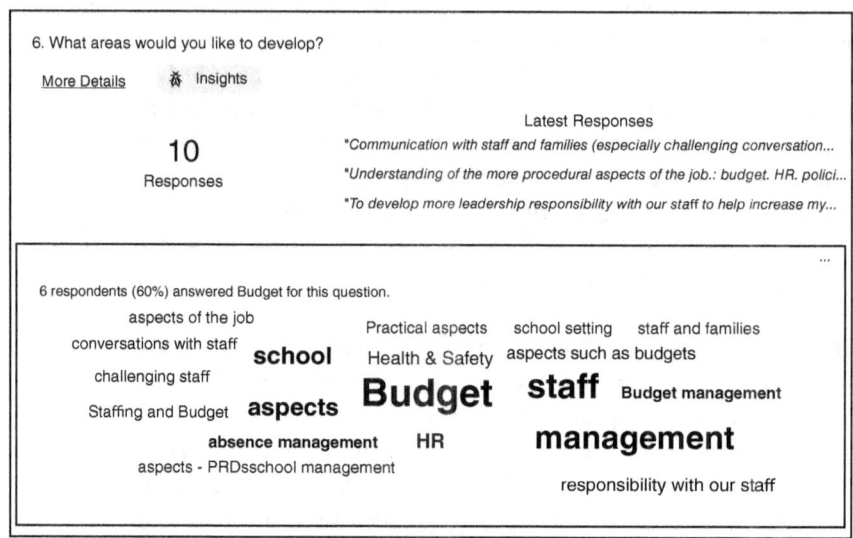

Figure 18.2 Development areas identified at the start of the programme

Course implementation

There were six mandatory sessions, The first session was held at the end of the January, and I asked that applicants and their headteachers attended together to establish the framework and explain the working model. This was the only session where both headteacher and deputy headteachers were in attendance, but I wanted to make sure we set clear boundaries and expectations of follow-up and support within the workplace environment.

In addition to the six mandatory sessions, we provided professional learning for both the headteacher and the depute in coaching and offered some clear direction in relation to the course, as follows:

- We deliberately focused the coaching training on strengthening the partnerships, and the depute headteachers began by working in pairs with their heads and asking them for their favourite examples of challenging or unexpected situations where they felt out of their depth. This set the correct dynamic and fostered an open learning culture.

- Each session provided input on key practical areas and focused on building the confidence of the depute headteachers.
- Ample time was allocated for peer discussion, within the context of the provision of a safe space.
- The crucial element was when the attendees returned to school, and heads all agreed to hold coaching conversations as a way of reflecting on the input they had provided in the first session. In Session 3, for example, we had a focus on finance with numerous workshops run by our business manager teams. When deputes returned to their schools, we asked that they reviewed their own staffing return and year-end budgets with their headteachers, taking their learning into the conversations.
- The model in Figure 18.1 outlines the key principles for the programme and places coaching conversations at the centre of the cycle to ensure learning is reflected on in a relevant and authentic context. *'Teachers who are reflective systematically collect evidence from their practice, allowing them to rethink and potentially open themselves to new interpretations'* (Attard & Armour, 2005, pp. 195–207).
- No formal assignment was required but the penultimate session was held in Edinburgh University Library as feedback highlighted to the *Into Headship* programme was that there was the perception that teachers felt disconnected from academia and that the familiarity with the physical environment is important in removing psychological barriers to achievement.

Impact of the course programme

The first module of the course programme had been established with a baseline and a focus on participants' confidence in relation to the role of headship. This lens provided a clear rubric to measure impact on confidence levels for headship in the short term and for the duration of and at the end of the six-week programme. Ultimately, measuring the long-term success of the course will become clearer when we are able to look at the proportion of depute headteachers taking part in the course programme who apply for and who remain in headship. This longitudinal analysis will take time.

The results, illustrated in Figures 18.3 and 18.4, show a growing confidence in becoming a headteacher, with the initial level of confidence of 2.3 out of 5 rising to 3.09 at the end of the six-month period. Given the small number in the cohort and relatively short timescales, this is positive.

As the course was a pilot, the first of its kind, I evaluated the impact using confidence and knowledge questionnaires. This data was also used to inform next steps. The feedback was overwhelmingly positive. The intention was never to 'force' people into applying to become a headteacher, in fact. the opposite. It was to help aspirant leaders to more fully understand the nature of the role and to identify if it was a route that they would wish to pursue. Figure 18.4 shows impact in

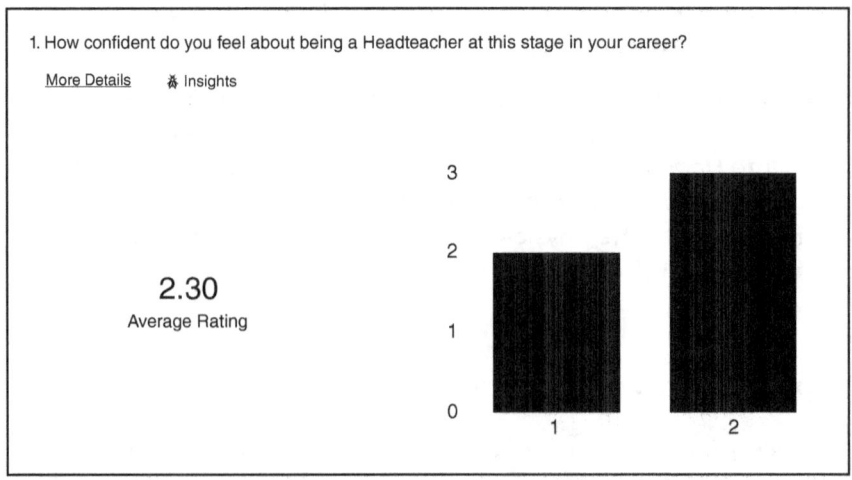

Figure 18.3 Confidence in becoming a headteacher: start of course programme

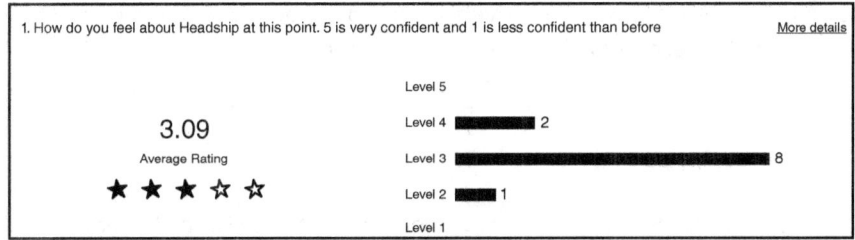

Figure 18.4 Confidence in becoming a headteacher: end of the course

terms of the average confidence rating put to participants at the end of the six weeks.

Clearly, much more lies behind these headline figures, but, overall, there was an increased level of confidence expressed by those depute headteachers who took part in the course. I plan to revisit participants at the end of this academic year, giving them one full year on to reflect.

Conclusion

Overall, the aim of the course was to focus on the process of developing headteachers; it was always envisaged as a journey of professional development. There will be many measures of impact at a small scale, and it is clear, at national level, that succession planning for leaders in schools is essential. While the course is only one small part of this, linking learning and promoting headship as an aspiration elevates the role. Feedback from participants was positive about the benefits of headteacher input; they were carefully selected and provided motivation, support, and inspiration. In summary, when we are thinking about organisational effectiveness, developing future leaders is an essential element. Getting the right people in the right jobs, in the right zone for development is not easy. As advisers, we are adept at listening, watching and identifying gaps, and when combined with quantitative and qualitative data, this can guide us through complexity. I learned a lot in designing the programme, and this year we have accepted fewer people on the course, with more focus and more space to unpack inputs and more support to guide valuable conversations. Effectively developing people is always an essential element of organisational development.

 Further reading

Greany, T. (2018) *Sustainable Improvement in Multi-School Groups: Research Report*. UCL Institute of Education/University of Nottingham.

Hargreaves, A., & Shirley, D. (2009) *The Fourth Way: The Inspiring Future for Educational Change*. San Francisco: Corwin Press.

 References

Attard, K., & Armour, K. M. (2005) Learning to become a learning professional: Reflections on one year of teaching. *European Journal of Teacher Education*, 28(2), 195–207.

Education Scotland (2022) *National Into Headship Evaluation Report*. Written by Professor Alma Harris. Online at: https://education.gov.scot/media/2336/into-headship-evaluation-report-alma-harris-sept-22.pdf. (Accessed on 24/08/25).

19 Transforming education through visionary leadership and effective organisational development

LES WALTON CBE

Key learning

- To achieve highly effective organisational development, education advisers and leaders need to fully understand and embrace PESTLE – the political, economic, social, technological, legal and environmental – drivers of change.

- An analysis of PESTLE will, in turn, help to inform the organisation's planning, people and performance needs and how these might best be aligned to achieve optimum success.

- Education advisers are well-placed to support leaders in an evaluation of a framework for and some of the key components of organisational development, such as strategic planning, curriculum, job design, professional growth, climate and systems analysis, and their impact on performance.

AoEA criteria

- Criterion 21: Understands the PESTLE drivers for change

- Criterion 22: Critically evaluates the design of the curriculum or educational offer

- Criterion 23: Is able to link vision, policy, strategy, plans, goals and ambitions to long-term requirements and immediate needs

- Criterion 24: Links the job design and people development to strategic requirements

- Criterion 27: Is able to assess the context for organisational improvement

Introduction

In today's rapidly changing world, the education sector faces challenges that demand transformative leadership, which, in turn, will help to transform schools. From managing evolving strategy to developing groundbreaking educational experiences, leaders in education play a vital role in empowering learners, motivating staff, and ensuring that their organisations flourish.

What separates great leaders from good ones is their ability to harness a diverse range of competencies and turn them into actionable strategies that inspire progress, innovation, and excellence. What separates great advisers from good ones is their ability to support and enable leaders in their endeavours to thrive.

This chapter delves into some essential skills every education leader needs and considers how these might be applied in developing successful, forward-looking schools. The school leader is at its heart. Support for leaders and the development of their organisations are, therefore, key in an education adviser's work with their schools. The AoEA uses the model as illustrated in Figure 19.1 as a key point of reference for organisational development advisers to apply in their work with school leaders and education providers. Subsequent sections of this chapter cover each of the component parts of the model, beginning with a focus on the PESTLE external drivers of change.

Thriving in complexity: mastering an understanding of the PESTLE drivers for change

The modern educational landscape is shaped by political, environmental, social, technological, legal, and economic (PESTLE) forces that continually impact on the status quo. Successful leaders do not just adapt to these changes, they anticipate and harness them to deliver unparalleled success.

Education leaders must have regard to the political direction, to the influence of, for example, the secretary of state for education, relevant ministers, civil servants, regulatory agencies and regional and local

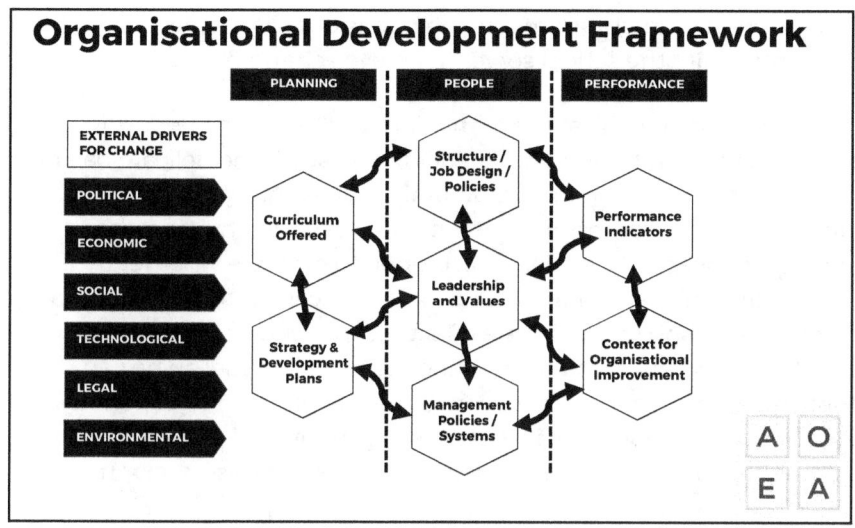

Figure 19.1 AoEA model for organisational development

authorities, whose decisions directly affect policy, governance, and funding. Understanding these wider political priorities enables leaders to align their own organisations with what an evolving system of schools needs.

With new legislation and funding arrangements continuously reshaping the education environment, leaders must stay ahead of the curve to keep their schools compliant, solvent, and, above all, thriving in the best interests of their young people.

The ability to decode the PESTLE dynamics is not just a skill, it is key to leaders guiding their schools and communities through the complexities of today's world with confidence and success.

Revolutionising learning: evaluating curriculum design and the educational offer

The heart of any successful school lies in its curriculum. It is more than a framework; it is the lifeblood and foundation of the learning experience. Great leaders understand the critical need to assess whether their curriculum meets the needs of both learners as well as the community the school serves in an ever-changing world.

This means ensuring that the curriculum and learning needs drive the deployment of finite resource. Leaders must strike the delicate balance between structural and non-structural costs, ensuring resources are directed towards fostering exceptional learning environments and experiences, with leaders called upon to evaluate whether their curriculum is truly fit for a young person's success in the modern era, whether teaching strategies are effective, and whether the staffing structures are both cost-effective and impactful. Leaders who can confidently answer these questions pave the way for innovation whilst sustaining operational excellence. The organisational development adviser has a key role to play in assisting leaders in this development.

From vision to success: linking goals, strategy, and action

At the core of exceptional leadership is the ability to inspire through compelling vision and strategy. Great leaders dare to dream big. They set their sights on world-class outcomes for learners and translate these ambitions into reality.

To transform vision into action, leaders must be maestros in their strategic planning. This involves working with their staff in the setting of SMART priorities – specific, measurable, achievable, relevant, and time-bound – while ensuring accountability structures are clear and firmly in place. It is not enough to have a roadmap; effective leaders ignite a sense of urgency within their teams, driving a focus on both short-term needs and long-term goals.

By mastering the art of linking vision, mission, policy, resources, and goals, educational leaders chart the path towards a brighter future, ensuring that the organisation's ambitions and aspirations become a living reality.

Empowering teams: job design and professional growth

Behind every high-performing organisation is a strong team, and behind every strong team is a leader who understands the need to engage that team and provide the necessary clarity in job role and design and in supporting further professional growth.

A key responsibility of leaders is to evaluate whether their organisation's leadership and staffing structures align with its strategic objectives. Beyond structural reviews and planned programmes of professional development, leaders must foster a culture of 'learning on the job' all day, every day, and where professional learning is a continuous journey that all staff are inspired to embrace.

Succession planning is equally crucial. Leaders have a key role to play in identifying and in nurturing future leaders within their teams, ensuring continuity in times of change. Through strategic job design and an unwavering commitment to staff development and professional growth, education leaders should seek to cultivate a workforce that is adaptable, motivated, and prepared to rise to any challenge.

Mastering efficiency: analysing management procedures and systems

Running an educational organisation is akin to piloting a ship: every system and procedure must work in harmony if it is to be steered towards success. Leadership plays a critical role in ensuring that systems and processes enable leaders to lead and teachers to teach to optimum effect. Conversely, by identifying inefficiencies and addressing them, leaders can create more learner-led, agile institutions ready to meet both immediate needs and future demands. Analytical expertise isn't just an asset. It is a necessity for leaders tasked with building sharply focused and successful organisations.

Defining success: measuring performance and growth

Outcomes matter but while examination scores and attendance figures often dominate the headlines, true, sustainable success goes far deeper. Effective leaders understand the value of both 'hard' and 'soft' measurement in painting a comprehensive picture of organisational effectiveness since one cannot be sustained without the other.

Hard data, inclusive of academic results, inspection dashboards, and national comparisons, forms an enticing foundation for evaluating success. However, equally important is to discern a comprehensive understanding of what has led to this endpoint. Insights from student, parent, and staff feedback, along with observational evidence, provide leaders with a more nuanced understanding of their institution's strengths and areas for improvement.

By combining these sources of intelligence, leaders can design well-rounded strategies that drive growth whilst addressing the unique needs of their communities. Success is not about just meeting statistical benchmarks but creating meaningful, lasting change.

Shaping culture: assessing the leadership's impact on climate

Leadership doesn't exist in a vacuum. It reverberates throughout the organisation, shaping its climate and, over time, its culture. From student engagement to staff morale, a leader's style and values influence every aspect of an organisation's performance. Exceptional leaders know how to assess the organisational climate and identify opportunities for improvement. By fostering an environment of collaboration, trust, and shared purpose, they create spaces where everyone feels valued and empowered to excel.

Moreover, great leaders adapt their leadership styles to meet the needs of their teams. Whether it's through transformational, servant, or situational leadership, they recognise that flexibility, though with a constancy of purpose, is the key to unlocking an organisation's full potential.

Conclusion

Educational leadership is not for the faint-hearted. It demands vision, adaptability, and an unwavering commitment to excellence. However, the rewards are profound: empowered and successful students, motivated staff, and organisations that not only meet expectations but exceed them.

Through mastering the competencies outlined here, which range from understanding what drives change to shaping effective organisational climate and culture, education advisers can support leaders in rising to the challenges of an evolving education system and leave an indelible mark on the future. The journey may be complex, but for those ready to embrace it, the possibilities are limitless. Step forward, support and enable leaders to thrive with moral courage and purpose, and assist in transforming an education system into a force that really does change lives.

Conclusions: Reflections on Book 4: *Advising on Organisational Development in Education*

DR TONY BIRCH AND IAN LANE

Arthur Jones, former editor of *Fortune* magazine, made the comment that successful organisations are perfectly aligned to get the results they get. The implication being that current performance is a product of the existing strategy, people and processes. If organisations want to improve, they need to adapt the way they work, to learn. In essence, this is the rationale for organisational development (OD) and, perhaps, helps to explain why many successful organisations embrace 'continuous improvement' as an approach. OD is easy to propose but much harder to bring about and consequently sustain, yet the 19 chapters that comprise this book demonstrate the richness, complexity, variety and, importantly, optimism associated with OD in education and include examples from England, Northern Ireland, Scotland and Wales.

The AoEA criteria for OD provide a guide to the knowledge, skills and expertise needed by the organisational development adviser (ODA) and are now the lens for this concluding chapter.

Understand the PESTLE drivers for change

PESTLE (political, economic, social, technological, legal and environmental) analysis is a well-established tool for the ODA and used across a range of sectors. Its main value as a tool for organisations is that it helps them to critically consider the external factors that influence their context. Using the headings systematically to comprehensively gather and analyse the forces influencing the organisation enable it to plan and prioritise. Ian Lane's chapter addresses this explicitly and demonstrates how a carefully constructed process can help to illuminate key development points. Three examples from Peter Lauener (political), Al Kingsley (technological) and Joanne Davison (legal) offer us insights into why understanding external pressures should influence strategy but also why taking a principled and evidenced, rather than deterministic, approach helps ensure those influences are used, ultimately, to the benefit of children and young people.

Can critically evaluate the design of the curriculum or educational offer

A central role of any educational organisation is the design of its educational offer. While this happens in a constantly changing environment: national priorities, inspection frameworks, children and young people's interests and motivations, available finance, these factors all serve to shape educational priorities and practices. Values guide us, too, and Carolyn Roberts' chapter is instructive here: the Framework for Ethical Leadership in Education is one tool that helps to ensure that decisions are based in sound principles.

The pair of chapters from Narinder Gill and Kevin McDermid illustrate that designing and implementing the curriculum is a multi-dimensional process and along with Matthew Humphreys account of developing the *Curriculum for Wales*, their insightful perspectives offer complementary views for the ODA in relation to strategy, people, processes and performance.

Ultimately, the educational offer is the 'why' of OD by defining the value of any provision for children and young people; the ODA's ability to critically evaluate and shape its design is vital.

Can link vision, policy, strategy, plans, goals and ambitions to long-term and immediate needs

In Peter Parish's chapter, he sets out a framework for organisational development that includes a series of key dimensions: curriculum offer; strategy and development plans; structure, job design and policies; leadership and values; management, policies and systems; performance indicators; and the Context for Organisational Improvement. It is in the connection between these elements, when they form a unified whole, that organisations become coherent and realise their vision. Several chapters demonstrate work to this effect: the co-ordinating leadership approach of Liz Birchenall in an English initial teacher education context and of Matthew Humphreys' account of *Curriculum for Wales*; the development of SEND provision through partnership in Kirsty Logan-Hall's account from Northern Ireland; and the developmental approach of Sian Smith in supporting schools in disadvantaged contexts – each chapter demonstrates the importance of co-ordinating vision, policy, strategy, plans, goals and ambitions through an OD approach.

Can link job design and people development to strategic requirements

People matter enormously in OD. Engaging the passion and energy of teachers, for example, is essential to school improvement – it is Michael Fullan's point: '*Educational change depends upon what teachers do and think. It is as simple and complex as that*' (Fullan, 2001, p. 115). The chapters in this volume focus on the engagement, development and impact of 'people'.

David Hargreaves (2001) proposed a model of human capital: the specific skills, experience and capabilities that exist individually and collectively within the education system connect and, in so doing, become even more powerful. Roisin Harbinson articulates the impact of designing and building the right leadership team for the right place, while Grant Gillies recognises that recruiting headteachers can be challenging but through a collaborative approach to addressing a clearly evidenced need, it can be met. Catherine Redgrave's chapter, too, is rooted firmly in a relational approach where trust was established and mutual understanding emerged from action. People and their capacities are at the heart of an ODA's work.

Is able to analyse management procedures and systems

Procedures and systems provide structure and efficiency to organisations: they help to co-ordinate routines and manage complex operations, being particularly important in areas such as safeguarding and finance. A key to their efficacy is that they are fit for purpose. Catherine Wegwermer, Harry Greer, Damian Eannetta and Jackie Wallace's account of the journey in Northern Ireland through *Pathways Into Partnership* includes a recognition that procedures and systems need to be aligned, but they recognise in their account how, in building voluntary partnerships, one size does not fit all. There needed to be a flexible framework to act as an enabler and for accountability purposes.

Can select and apply a variety of measurements of success and performance indicators

A key part of the ODA's role is to offer an honest and realistic appraisal of performance. Three chapters illustrate how evidence from measurement and performance indicators can act as guides for action. Firstly, Kirsty Logan-Hall's chapter illustrates how evidence can form the basis of action. She describes the growing demand for SEND provision in Northern Ireland. By delving deep into the evidence around this growth and understanding the needs of families, an approach has been developed which is both sensitive to context and sustainable. The challenge of implementing a new curriculum described by Matthew Humphreys – *Curriculum for Wales* – was designed to raise standards, and by understanding the patterns in its implementation, leaders were able to prioritise and pinpoint actions. Sian Smith's approach is evidence informed; she uses it to both understand the issues and develop approaches which then enable people to transcend their current situations and make a difference to the achievement of disadvantaged pupils.

Liz Birchenall's contribution recognises that there is often not one measure of a successful organisation but several. She describes key drivers for her initial teacher education programme, the way they influenced thinking and how they responded as an organisation, ultimately combining these to secure successful inspection outcomes. Emma Knights' chapter is an important reminder of the impact governance can have on OD, particularly when it takes responsibility for strategy. Her emphasis is on collaboratively building a well-informed, focused and carefully prioritised strategy that improves performance.

Is able to assess the impact of leadership on the context for organisational improvement

Leaders carry huge responsibilities and manage a complex interplay of plans, intentions and actions from multiple people, which research evidence confirms as important. David Hopkins (2024) noted that the leading education systems around the world help to sustain their improvement by developing and nurturing future leaders. On a small scale, this is the purpose of Grant Gillies' strategy – to develop future headteachers. Perhaps, this is Michael Fullan's point when he argues: *'Ultimately, your leadership in a culture of change will be judged effective or ineffective not by who you are as a leader but by what leadership you produce in others'* (2001, p. 137).

How we analyse and understand leadership is a complex process – often educational organisations are judged by outcomes, so Peter Parish, Ian Lane and Les Walton offer another perspective through the Context for Organisational Improvement model. Here 'lead' indicators are identified and measured, giving important information about the climate of the organisation.

Les Walton's chapter exploring the concept of transformational leadership and its implications for ODAs is an important conclusion to this volume. He advises that the ODA should:

> *Step forward, support and enable leaders to thrive with moral courage and purpose, and assist in transforming an education system into a force that really does change lives.*

Conclusion

ODAs must root themselves in time, place and people. Attuning themselves to context, they advise on strategy, people, processes and performance. Organisational development in education should be ambitious for children and young people, optimistic in outlook, spirited in nature, embracing external change forces, enabling organisations to thrive. Then, as Roisin Harbinson comments in her chapter:

> *By honouring the dignity and equality of those whose life we touch and by not placing limitations on the group, the journey should end at the destination we plan – or maybe somewhere even more exciting.*

 References

Fullan, M. (2001) *The New Meaning of Educational Change*. London: Routledge.

Hargreaves, D. (2001) A capital theory of school effectiveness and improvement. *British Educational Research Journal*, 27(4), 487–503.

Hopkins, D. (2024) *Unleashing Greatness: A Strategy for School Improvement*. Woodbridge, England: John Catt Educational.

The following table summarises the learning that this book brings together:

Criterion	Key learning	Chapters
21. Understands the PESTLE drivers for change	The educational landscape is shaped by the political, environmental, social, technological, legal and economic (PESTLE) drivers for change that continually impact on schools and their education providers. Successful leaders do not just adapt to these changes; instead, they anticipate and harness them to deliver unparalleled success. The organisational development adviser (ODA) has a key role to play in supporting leaders in understanding the potential impact of PESTLE on their organisations with a view to enabling a proactive response.	1, 2, 3, 5, 7, 8, 11, 13, 16, 19
22. Critically evaluates the design of the curriculum or educational offer	The ODA has a key role to play in supporting schools or groups of schools in an evaluation and design of their curriculum. Education advisers can assist in asking the right questions and in enabling an effective and systematic approach to curriculum design, which is both learner-led and affordable.	3, 6, 8, 9, 10, 12, 16, 17, 18, 19

→

23. Is able to link vision, policy, strategy, plans, goals and ambitions to long-term requirements and immediate needs	The key to effective organisational development planning is to ensure the alignment of curriculum; strategy and development plans; structure, job design and policies; leadership and values; management, policies and systems; performance indicators; and the Context for Organisational Improvement. It is in the connection between these elements, when they form a unified whole, that organisations become coherent and realise their vision. The ODA can assist leaders in ensuring that this is the case.	1 2 3 4 5 6 7 8 9 10 11 12 13 14 15 17 19
24. Links the job design and people development to strategic requirements	ODAs have a key role to play in helping to make sure that people are at the heart of an organisation's development. Recruiting, retaining and investing in ongoing professional learning to ensure that leaders and their staff have both the specialist skills and means to deliver to evolving need is a key ingredient in an organisation's continuous improvement.	3 4 6 7 8 9 11 12 14 18 19

→

25. Is able to analyse management procedures and systems	Procedures and systems matter. They provide structure and efficiency to organisations and help to co-ordinate routines and manage complex operations, in areas such as curriculum design, safeguarding and finance. Systems are at play in all areas of a school's or group of schools' working practice. Key to an effective system is its fitness for purpose, and the education adviser has a key role to play in supporting leaders to ensure that both their systems' design and procedures enable rather than inhibit organisational effectiveness.	3 4 6 7 8 10 14
26. Is able to apply a variety of measurements of success and performance indicators	A key part of the ODA's role is to offer an honest and realistic appraisal of a school's or group of schools' performance. In this respect, not just the results but those key performance indicators that are most applicable to an individual school's context. Some of those measures will be shaped by national policy, but all should be tailored to individual learner needs.	3 5 6 8 14 15 16
27. Is able to assess the context for organisational improvement	Organisational context, or climate as it is often referred to, significantly influences workplace culture and performance. Leadership and the ODA in support of leadership can help to shape this context, positively impacting on staff morale, teamwork and overall efficiency. A positive context fosters collaboration and motivation, leading to high levels of performance, whereas a negative one can lead to disengagement, inefficiency and, as a result, a less effective organisation.	3 4 5 8 9 11 13 14 15 17 18 19

As illustrated in all four books in the series *'The Education Adviser'*, the influence of and the difference made by education advisers as they seek to empower the leaders and governors with whom they work in enabling effective change isn't to be underestimated or understated. The well thought out and careful deployment of advisers will assist any organisation in striving to continuously improve, no matter their size, complexity or jurisdiction.

> *The vision of the AoEA is that every school, college, and education provider has access to high quality support, advice and challenge, which is independent and focused on improving outcomes for children, schools, and their communities.*
>
> (AoEA website, 2025)

Index

Note: Page numbers in *italic* indicate a figure and page numbers in **bold** indicate a table on the corresponding page.

action 192; action planning 68–69; case for 182–183; translating beliefs and values into 75–77; vision into action across the system 77–78
advisers: areas to explore 88, 89, 90; education 38–39; as facilitator for change 60–61
advisory relationship 127–128
advisory strategies 102–103, 126–127
affordability, curriculum 109–112, *110*
aligning planning, people and performance 83–94
ambitions 197–198
art of the possible 32–39
assessing impact of leadership 152–159; on climate 194; on context for organisational improvement 200
Association of Education Advisors 3–5; criteria 21, 32, 40, 51, 57, 64, 73, 83, 95, 106, 114, 124, 133, 145, 152, 161, 169, 179, 189

behaviours, collaborative 175
beliefs 75–77
benchmarking 112
board, the 15, 48, 133, 135, 137–140

case studies: deputes 179–188; PESTLE 26–30, *28*; quality of SEND provision 73–79
challenges 70–71, 181–182
change 181; adviser as facilitator for 60–61; building the case for 59–60; context of significant national change 64–71; digital as lever for 43–45; making sense of the changing rules of the game 162; managing risks of structural change 51–56; maintaining ethos and values through 48; organisational development as foundation for 42–43; PESTLE drivers for 190–191, 196–197; sustaining change when you're not in the room 102–103
climate, assessing leadership's impact on 194
co-creation, curriculum as 98–100, *99*
coherence 102
collaboration 45–46, 169–177
comfort zones, working beyond 57–63
communication 68, 138; lack of 54
compassionate curriculum 95–104, *99*, *101*
competencies 44
complexity 190–191
confidence 44
context 89, 97–98; case study 26–30, *28*; for change 181; contextual understanding 101; developing initial teacher training provider 64–71; future-proofing with PESTLE 21–31, *22*; managing risks of structural change 51–56; organisational development in 6–7, 10–13; for organisational improvement 200; quality of SEND provision 73–79; responding to and working with political change 32–39; technological 40–49; working beyond comfort zones 57–63
Context for Organisational Improvement (COI) 152–159
continuation stage 69–71
continuous improvement 47, 102
control 96–97
culture: of the organisation 138–140, *140*; shaping 194
curriculum 95–104, *99*, *101*; affordability 109–112, *110*; content 108–109; design 69, 88, 98, 106–112, 191–192; intent 107–108; plan 110

data 61
decisions: failure to make difficult decisions 55–56
deep contextual understanding 101
delegation 69
Department for Education (DfE) 65–71, 134, 139–140
deputes 179–188
DfE see Department for Education (DfE)
digital: citizenship 44–45; as lever for change 43–45; strategy 43–44
direction: agreeing 128–129; lack of 53–54
disadvantage see socio-economic disadvantages
diverse system of schools 169–177

education, transformation of 189–195
education advisers 3–6, 21–22, 32–33, 36–39, 62, 152–153, 189–190
educational offer 191–192, 197
educational provision, setting up 90–93
education service realignment 90
effective curriculum 95–104, *99*, *101*; design 106–112
effective organisational development; empowering leaders through 161–167; transforming education through 189–195
effective senior leadership team 114–123
efficiency 193
empowering leaders 161–167
empowering teams 16, 193
environment 97–98
ethical leadership 145–151
ethos 48, 116–117
evaluating curriculum design 191–192, 197
existing systems 70–71

feedback 69, 130
financial stewardship 46
focused framework 100
Framework for Ethical Leadership in Education (FELE) 14, 145–149, 151, 197
future-proofing 21–25, *22*, 31; case study 26–30, *28*; PESTLE analysis process 25–26, *26*

goals 192, 197–198
governance 47–48, 133–141
growth 45–46; measuring 194

headteachers 179–188

ICFP *see* integrated curriculum and financial planning (ICFP)
immediate needs 197–198
impact 103–104, 175–177, 186–187; assessing impact of climate 194; assessing impact of leadership 152–159, 200; deputes 179–188; empowering leaders 161–167; importance of ethical leadership 145–151; structured approach to collaboration 169–178; transforming education 189–195
implementation 183–185; phases of 101–102; stage of 69
inclusive curriculum 95–104, *99*, *101*
influence 96–97
initial teacher training provider 64–71
integrated curriculum and financial planning (ICFP) 13, 106, 109, *110*, 111–112

job design 87, 193, 198

key players 162–163
knowledge, lack of 53

leadership 15–16, 47–48, 96–97; assessing impact of 194, 200; deputes 179–188; empowering leaders 161–167; ethical 145–151; impact on Context for Organisational Improvement 152–159; recruiting 114–123; structured approach to collaboration 169–178; transforming education through 189–195
learners, well-being for 46
local authority education service realignment 90
long-term needs 197–198
long-term sustainability 46–47

management procedures and systems 193, 199
managing change, stages of 67–70, 67
managing curriculum design 106–112
managing risks 51–56
mandated changes 65–66, 66
materials: piloting 69
MATs see multi-academy trusts (MATs) 45–46
measurement: growth 194; performance 194, 199–200; success 199–200
modelling 75, 77, 92, 102, 117, 158
momentum 103
multi-academy trusts (MATs) 44–46, 48–49, 134–136

national change 64–71
national objectives 36–38
new educational provision, setting up 90–93
Northern Ireland 73–79, 169–177

organisational development (OD): in action 7–8; aligning of planning, people and performance 85–86, 90–94, **91–92**; in context 6–7; developing initial teacher training provider 64–71; empowering leaders through 161–167; ethical leadership and 145–151; future-proofing with PESTLE 21–31; governance and 133–141; managing risks of structural change 51–56; quality of SEND provision 73–79; responding to and working with political change 32–39; technological 40–49; transforming education through 189–195; working beyond comfort zones 57–63
organisational development adviser (ODA) 8–11, 84, 106, 190, 192, 196–197, 200–204
organisational effectiveness: aligning planning, people and performance 83–94; curriculum 95–104, 106–112; governance 133–141; planning for 13–15; recruiting senior leadership team 114–123; socio-economic disadvantage 124–131
organisational goals 42–44, 153–154, 157

organisational improvement: impact of leadership styles on 157–159, 200; role of leadership in 157
outcomes 166–167, 175–177

partnership, impact of 62
pedagogy 102
people 54–55, 83–87, 85–86, 97–98, 198; applying the organisational development 90–94, **91–92**; context for organisational development 89–90; management policies and systems 87–88; and the performance strand 89; and the planning strand 88–89; structure, job design and policies 87; support the development of 129–130
performance 15–16; aligning planning, people and 83–94; Context for Organisational Improvement 152–159; deputes 179–188; empowering leaders 161–167; importance of ethical leadership 145–151; measuring 194, 199–200; structured approach to collaboration 169–178; transforming education 189–195
PESTLE 21–25, 22, 31, 190–191, 196–197; analysis process 25–26, 26; case study 26–30, 28
PGCE see University of Manchester (UoM) primary postgraduate certificate of education (PGCE)
phases of implementation 101–102
piloting materials 69
place 97–98
plans 197–198; sharing 128–129
planning 13–15; action planning 68–69; aligning people, performance and 83–94; curriculum 95–104, 106–112; governance 133–141; recruiting senior leadership team 114–123; socio-economic disadvantage 124–131
policies 87, 197–198; management 87
political change 32–39
priorities, identification of 126–127

professional growth 193
programme self-evaluation 68–69
progression 102
purpose 96

quality: good outcomes follow quality practice 166–167; of SEND provision 73–79

recruiting 114–123
resistance 103
resources 137
responsibilities of governance 133–141; see also governance
revolutionising learning 191–192
risks 51–56, 181–182

safeguarding 44–45
schools, system of 21, 23, 73–79, 169–178, 191
school setting: quality of SEND provision 73–79; socio-economic disadvantage 124–131; structured approach to collaboration 169–177
self-evaluation 68–69
SEND provision 27, 73–79, 198–199
senior leadership team 114–123
service offer 88
shared truths 128
sharing the plan 128–129
skills, collaborative 175
smaller-scale initiatives 93–94
society, transformation of 32–36
socio-economic disadvantage 124–131
Special Educational Needs and Disabilities (SEND) see SEND provision
staff: building confidence and competencies 44; staff deployment analysis 110–111; well-being for 46
strategic cycle, key steps in 136–140, *140*
strategic direction 135–136
strategic focus 133–141
strategic plan 83–94

strategic priorities 137
strategic requirements 198
strategy 192, 197–198
Strengths, Weaknesses, Opportunities, Threats (SWOT) 27, 30, 88, 136
structural change 51–56
structure 87
structured approach to collaboration 169–177
student number projections 109
success 192; defining 194; indicators 89; measurements of 199–200
sustainability 46–47; curriculum 109–112, *110*
sustainable curriculum design 106–112
sustained focus 133–141
SWOT see Strengths, Weaknesses, Opportunities, Threats (SWOT)
systemic impact 96
system of schools 21, 23, 73–79, 169–178, 191
systems, management 87

teacher training see initial teacher training provider
technological context 40–49
time resources: managing change with limited resources 70
transformation 33–36; of education 189–195
truths, shared 128

University of Manchester (UoM) primary postgraduate certificate of education (PGCE) 64–72

values 48, 67–68; translating into action 75–77
vision 67–68, 75, 137–138, 192, 197–198; into action 77–78
visionary leadership 189–195

well-being 46
work packages 69

For Product Safety Concerns and Information please contact our EU representative GPSR@taylorandfrancis.com
Taylor & Francis Verlag GmbH, Kaufingerstraße 24, 80331 München, Germany

www.ingramcontent.com/pod-product-compliance
Lightning Source LLC
Chambersburg PA
CBHW060624250426
43670CB00056B/1959